The Consumer's Guide
to Earth Sheltered Housing

The Consumer's Guide to Earth Sheltered Housing

A Step-by-Step Workbook for Prospective Owners

Mary Rollwagen

with

Susan Taylor • T. Lance Holthusen

Illustrations by Katherine Reif Anderson

VNR Van Nostrand Reinhold Company

Printed in the United States of America
Designed by Ernie Haim

Published by Van Nostrand Reinhold Company Inc.
135 West 50th Street
New York, New York 10020

Van Nostrand Reinhold Company Limited
Molly Millars Lane
Wokingham, Berkshire RG11 2PY, England

Van Nostrand Reinhold
480 La Trobe Street
Melbourne, Victoria 3000, Australia

Macmillan of Canada
Division of Gage Publishing Limited
164 Commander Boulevard
Agincourt, Ontario M1S 3C7, Canada

16 15 14 13 12 11 10 9 8 7 6 5 4 3 2 1

Library of Congress Cataloging in Publication Data

Rollwagen, Mary.
   The consumer's guide to earth sheltered housing.

   Bibliography: p.
   Includes index.
   1. Earth sheltered houses. 2. Consumer education.
I. Taylor, Susan, 1941–   . II. Holthusen, T.
Lance, 1938–   . III. Anderson, Katherine Reif.
IV. Title.
TH4819.E27R64 1984   690'.8 83-16933
ISBN 0-442-26410-0

Contents

Foreword

When asked to write a foreword for this book, I thought of the many titles that have been written on the subject over the past few years: publications that present basic architectural and engineering design information and public policy information, the several major conference proceedings, and the many other design, construction, and how-I-did-it books.

Although almost all of these books will be of value to someone trying to design an earth sheltered house, many contain more information than is necessary for someone who is not a designer, contractor, or researcher. In fact, they may contain more information than can be appropriately used by an inexperienced layperson. The most successful and cost-effective earth sheltered projects are those that respond correctly, in overall design and in details, to specific site and climate situations. What may work best on a hillside in Portland may not be effective for a flat site in Oklahoma. The technical manuals cannot prepare the layperson for all the difficulties, opportunities, and trade-offs presented by the specific mixture of soil conditions, topography, and climate found on a particular site.

In addition, hardly any of these books have specifically addressed the plight of and information required by people who merely want to arrange to have an earth sheltered house built without becoming a design expert themselves.

This thoroughly practical manual approaches the undertaking of building an earth sheltered house from a uniquely different perspective. It is process oriented. It guides the reader through each stage of the plan/design/build process, emphasizing those elements that can and should be most directly influenced by the potential owner.

For instance, the authors' discussion of architect/ client and contractor/client relationships is geared to helping an owner define personal concepts of shelter and communicate such concepts clearly and efficiently to the professionals involved. Professional services can thus be used to the best and most cost-effective advantage. This process discussion would certainly be of benefit to any layperson building a custom house, whether earth sheltered or not.

In my opinion the construction of earth sheltered housing to date has been constrained far more by the lack of an experienced and reliable infrastructure for designing and building this type of housing than by any lack of interest. Although more avenues are available today to obtain an earth sheltered home, it is still an exercise fraught with many potential dangers for the uninitiated.

This book helps the new home builder anticipate the dangers and strongly suggests the appropriate use of professional guidance. Working through the activities presented in the text, the potential earth sheltered home owner should gain the confidence to take charge of as much of the creative and construction aspects of the project as is desired. I would, however, concur with the authors that in all cases experts should be consulted at least for such critical design and construction concerns as structural strength and waterproofing.

The suggestions throughout this book on where and how to look for professional assistance will make an owner's search for experts easier, but the truth of the matter is that knowledgeable architects, engineers, contractors, code officials, and lenders are still widely scattered. Having an earth sheltered house designed and built still entails, in some areas, a bit of pioneering and probably a lot of flexibility in putting together the right professional team.

In fact, this book suggests flexibility in many more decisions than just which experts to use. I agree with the authors' suggestions that alternatives also be considered for sites, materials, and even for designs.

The chief value of this book, it seems to me, is that choices appropriate for owners are outlined, choices more appropriate for experts are identified, and the differences between the two are made clear.

Achieving the right design and getting the house built the way it was designed, all for a reasonable price, are no small accomplishments. Taking the time to walk through all the steps first, by reading this book and doing the paperwork suggested, is a good way to avoid most of the pitfalls and finish with a safe, functional, and thoroughly satisfying home.

RAYMOND STERLING, *Director*
Underground Space Center
University of Minnesota

Preface

In the course of several years of organizing and managing conferences on earth sheltered construction, we at TLH Associates heard many common sense suggestions. We noticed, however, that conference audiences contained mostly providers: either professional designers and builders or do-it-yourself owner-builders.

Where were average new home buyers—those "lay" people who want new houses and want them to be energy efficient but have no intention of actually building their own house? They were not, certainly, at a conference learning how to apply waterproofing or design footings.

We realized that most people find education about earth sheltering pertinent only when the new house gleam appears in their eyes. They usually do not choose to learn how to *build* an earth sheltered house, but rather how to *have an earth sheltered house built*.

But where should a prospective owner begin? How does earth sheltering work? Does it cost more than an ordinary house? Where can experienced professionals be found? The questions multiply. Some seem too simple even to ask, and others yield answers

too technical to understand. Yet the potential pitfalls in an earth sheltered project are not always technical ones. To avoid problems, owners must grasp such subtleties as site selection criteria, correct approaches to lending institutions, and potential obstacles lurking in building codes or zoning ordinances.

As our awareness of the questions grew, so this book has grown into a step-by-step guide to the complete earth sheltered planning, designing and building process. The answers, we found, describe a process that is not so very different from that of having any custom house built.

We have developed a personal bias: earth sheltered design and construction need a professional's hand. Safety is the primary reason; next comes appropriateness of the design. For the three of us, though, a third reason for working with a good architect is the critical one: quality of design. In our opinion many current earth sheltered designs concentrate on energy savings and neglect aesthetics. We hope prospective owners reading this book will be encouraged to develop their imaginations and be satisfied only with a design that is nothing less than the best.

Acknowledgments

To my chagrin and hers, Sue Taylor's move to Pakistan prevented our joint authorship of this book from being fully realized. Without her energy and sense, the project could not have begun, and her long-distance assistance as the book took shape continued to be invaluable. To her and to T. Lance Holthusen, whose participation and cheerful support through a difficult period made the work seem possible, I offer my most grateful thanks.

TLH Associates, Inc., a company specializing in helping people and groups understand and shape their futures, graciously provided me not only a leave of absence to complete the book; more important, TLH supplied both a consistent framework of experience in interpreting and communicating technical information and a wide range of resources on which to draw.

Architect Ed Frenette, of Setter, Leach & Lindstrom Inc. in Minneapolis, helped more than he knows to shape the book and affirm its focus on professionalism as the means to safe and well-designed homes. I am also indebted to Brent Anderson for his patient explanations and willingness to share an extensive collection of construction photographs. Brent and Charles Lane, both formerly associated with the Underground Space Center at the University of Minnesota, supplied their characteristic blend of theoretical and practical knowledge of earth sheltering.

The thoroughness and common sense of Ray Sterling, the Underground Space Center's director, have contributed immeasurably to today's understanding of and appreciation for earth sheltering. His willingness to read the manuscript at a crucial stage and to contribute his thoughtful comments in the form of a foreword are deeply appreciated.

A simple thanks hardly seems adequate to those who read—and vastly improved—the manuscript: Marge Christensen, Jody Duclos, Molly LaBerge, Charles Pederson, Sarah Susanka, and the incomparable Malcolm Wells.

Acknowledging thankfully the word processor's magic, my appreciation for their assistance in the crunches go to Marge Christensen, Julie Gill, Dorothy McNaughton, and Julie Stroud.

Chapter 1

The Earth Sheltered Option

An earth sheltered house is protected by the earth and warmed by the sun. The growing appeal of this kind of architecture is perhaps explained by its simplicity. We instinctively respond with approval to the inherent common sense of earth sheltering.

The idea sounds simple, but its application is not. Building a good earth sheltered house involves much more than simply placing earth against walls and roof. Like most good, simple ideas, the practical realization of a successful earth project requires planning, skill, experience, and creativity.

Since the first wave of pioneering by do-it-yourselfers and a few professionals in the early 1970s, the concept of earth sheltering has attracted sufficient consumer and industry attention to move it into the mainstream of the home-building marketplace. Architects are finding ever more creative solutions to the design challenges of earth sheltering, suppliers are discovering new markets for their applicable products, contractors are learning the techniques, and new specialized earth sheltered building companies are emerging.

What this means is that earth sheltering is now a realistic alternative, not only for the do-it-yourself builder, but for anyone contemplating a new house.

In most parts of the country, consumers can now avail themselves of experienced and knowledgeable design and construction professionals. You may not be a pioneer, but you can still be in the second wave, taking advantage of all that has been learned earlier.

This book is designed for those second-wave consumers who may be interested in owning an earth sheltered house but have neither the skill nor the intention to pour their own concrete or create their own design. The understanding necessary to manage a successful project does not include knowing how to build the house; many "build your own earth shelter" books are available if you are so inclined. Rather, this book offers advice on how to approach the planning and decision making. In step-by-step sequence, we will describe the tasks involved in an earth sheltered project, paying particular attention to those that may or must be performed by you, the owner.

Relying on professionals for the tasks they do best does not mean relinquishing responsibility for the entire process. For a truly satisfying and successful building experience, the owner, as final decision maker, should understand the language and rationale of earth sheltering and be fully aware of its obstacles and opportunities. You must understand and communicate your needs clearly and know how to assess the resulting plans.

Our purpose is not to convince you that earth sheltering is the best strategy for an energy-conserving home. In fact, an understanding of its drawbacks, obstacles, or simple unsuitability under certain conditions might lead you to decide that earth sheltering is not for you. The proper time for such a decision is before, not after, launching a project. After all, earth sheltering is an alternative, not a religion.

The knowledge needed to plan a good project is presented in this book according to the sequence of activities and decisions occurring in most custom home building processes. Not every project will proceed exactly as the generalized one presented here, but by using the offered work space to record and check your progress, you will transform this generalized manual into a personalized account of your own project's development.

Briefly, the sequence of tasks discussed in the book is:

- Weighing the advantages and drawbacks of earth sheltering
- Learning how it works and what it looks like
- Evaluating your climate and location
- Checking codes and zoning
- Finding an appropriate site
- Identifying personal shelter needs and goals
- Assessing personal resources
- Choosing professional assistance
- Communicating with the architect
- Assessing the design
- Selecting a contractor
- Reassessing costs from estimates
- Acquiring financing
- Observing construction
- Final inspection and acceptance

A caution: some tasks may rearrange themselves and others may happen simultaneously in your own project. The sequence above outlines the flow of information in this book as well as a *possible* flow of work. Where certain tasks *must* be accomplished before others to avoid pitfalls, you will be alerted.

Evaluation

Evaluating earth sheltering will be difficult before you discover more specifically how it works. Never-

theless, you should retain some skepticism about earth sheltering as you continue reading this book, so being aware of the pros and cons from the outset will be helpful. You can always come back and reread this section after the terms become a little more familiar.

The Benefits of Earth Sheltered Housing

The benefits of earth sheltering that first attracted architectural attention were both aesthetic and practical. Conserving or re-creating open, natural environments, inhibiting excess water runoff, saving space in highly built-up areas, and intruding on the landscape as little as possible were the earliest goals. Architect Malcolm Wells sums up the advantages of earth sheltering in his early book of sketches and plans, *Underground Designs*, when he writes that integrating architecture more completely with landscape offers "a silent, green alternative to the asphalt society."

Saving energy is the advantage most earth sheltered home owners strive for today. Good earth sheltered design and construction, combined with passive solar features, can reduce fuel usage so dramatically that the addition of a wood-burning stove can make many houses nearly energy self-sufficient for heating. This reason alone is enough incentive for many people to build an earth sheltered home.

The experience of present earth sheltered owners bears out the claims of energy savings. Figure 1-1 charts cost data that were obtained in Oklahoma from actual utility billing records. Total energy usage (lighting and appliances as well as heating and cooling) in earth sheltered homes was compared to that of conventional aboveground homes. The "earth sheltered" line in the chart represents five typical

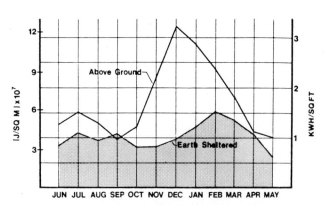

1—1. Monthly total energy usage in conventional aboveground and earth sheltered homes in Oklahoma.

(From Lester L. Boyer, Center for Natural Energy Design, Oklahoma State University. See Appendix B).

all-electric earth sheltered homes in the same location as the conventional homes. The total annual energy usage of the earth sheltered dwellings is approximately 40 percent lower. If only heating and cooling energy use were compared, the earth sheltered homes would show an even greater reduction in energy consumption.

There is a secondary plus to the energy benefits. Should an interruption in fuel supply or a power failure occur in cold weather, the temperature in an earth sheltered house will remain comfortable for days. It may never drop to a point where pipes would freeze: northern earth sheltered home owners can safely turn off the heat and go south for the winter.

In addition to providing you, the owner, with energy savings and self-sufficiency, an earth sheltered house offers other advantages that may be important to you.

- You may have increased yard space for your own pleasure, and you provide parklike views for your neighbors.
- The mass of earth surrounding the house deadens sound and vibrations; owners say their earth sheltered houses are remarkably quiet. They claim a sense of tranquility, security, and comfort.
- Most of the exterior shell of the house is encased in earth and thus requires little outside maintenance: no new siding, gutter cleaning, exterior painting.
- Because air infiltration is minimized, the interior is quite free of drafts and dust.
- With the choice of sturdy grasses and native plants, the landscape can require little maintenance.
- Masonry earth sheltered homes are less susceptible to fire risk than are conventional wood-frame houses; many owners have negotiated lower insurance rates. The masonry is rot-proof and termite-proof as well.
- Earth sheltered homes are protected from the ravages of hail, wind, tornadoes, and hurricanes. Surprisingly, they can be safer than aboveground structures even in earthquakes, since earthquake damage is primarily a result of the whipping action on the aboveground portions of buildings.

Beyond the personal benefits you derive from living in an earth sheltered home, there is satisfaction in knowing you are building in a manner that preserves the earth's surface and resources. Your earth sheltered home will reduce rainwater runoff and preserve green space. You can design so as to intrude as little as possible on the natural landscape. In addition, earth sheltering allows you to go a step further and reclaim land that is not otherwise usable, restoring it to a partially green state.

The Drawbacks of Earth Sheltered Housing

The first drawback to consider is the amount of your time it could take to have an earth sheltered home built. Of course, your time is absorbed by the building of any new home, but building an earth sheltered home should significantly increase the amount of attention you pay to predesign planning and detail in order to assure that a safe, comfortable home is built.

Architects and contractors in your community may be unfamiliar with earth sheltered construction. Though this drawback is less true today than it was just a few years ago, you may still have to search for experienced professionals or be prepared for your project to be the first lesson for an inexperienced one.

Finding the right professionals is one problem; satisfying other professionals could be another. Satisfying the building codes officials, for example, could be time-consuming and expensive if unforeseen objections to your proposed design are raised.

Inevitably, it seems, the challenge of finding financing could prove to be the biggest obstacle of all. In many communities where earth sheltered construction is new, lenders need careful reassurance that the concept of earth sheltering, and your project in particular, is worthy of investment. A very professional approach to a lender is a necessity and will require some homework.

Other features of earth sheltered housing also make it an inappropriate alternative in certain situations.

- A contractor inexperienced in earth sheltered construction is likely to bid higher in the first place to cover some trial and error. He may have to rip out and do things over again, and the rather complex scheduling requirements of earth sheltering invite the possibility of costly delays.
- If adequate supplies of materials like concrete plank or proper soil for backfilling are not available nearby, there may be long waits and high shipping charges.
- Sites with difficult access or adverse subsurface

1—2. An example of an earth sheltered house built from standard or "stock" plans in Forest Lake, MN, by Earth Shelter Corporation of America, a construction company that builds only earth sheltered homes (see Appendix B).

conditions are either totally unsuited for earth sheltering or else the cause of formidable additional cost.

- An earth sheltered house may not look very much like older aboveground houses in the neighborhood, a definite drawback in the appraiser's view. In a subdivision restrictive covenants may be in effect that would eliminate earth sheltering as an available design choice.

The above discussion is an attempt to dissuade you from building an earth sheltered home if it is incompatible with your situation. As you read through the next chapters, you will discover more specifically what we mean. It is easy to get carried away with the novelty of the idea or the image you want to project and thus lose sight of your real shelter goals, needs, and conditions.

Cost Comparison with Conventional Housing

Cost of Construction: Does earth sheltering cost more than a conventional house? This question has no simple answer. The concept is still too new: not enough houses have been built to make generalizations valid, and nearly all that have been built to date are one-of-a-kind models whose costs per square foot can be computed in so many ways as to skew normal comparisons.

Comparing apples to apples brings an answer somewhat closer. Assuming earth sheltered houses are custom designed and thus comparing their cost to conventional custom-designed houses, relative costs range from being equal to 25 percent higher.

When earth sheltered homes are built with more of the economies of mass-produced houses, that is, with repeated use of the same design and methods, the range of cost difference will certainly narrow. In fact, several earth sheltered building companies do offer these economies. The owner chooses a model from standardized designs, and it is built with methods that have been used over and over. These companies claim their houses can be built as quickly and cheaply as conventional houses (see Appendix B).

Life-Cycle Costs: Before the 1970s, people usually assumed that the initial cost of a house was the only cost that mattered. Since the oil embargo and the onset of high interest rates, however, we are all beginning to realize that the purchase price is only a part of the equation. The total costs over the life of a house also include ongoing financing, maintenance, and utility costs. A larger front-end investment that will reduce the ongoing costs may therefore be a prudent one.

Comparing the life-cycle costs of earth sheltered and conventional houses is somewhat risky, since an accurate comparison relies on assumptions about hard-to-predict variations in future interest rates and energy costs. In fact, the increase in interest rates over the past several years has added even more to the life costs of houses than has the increase in energy prices.

In the past the life-cycle cost comparisons that were based on 9 percent interest rates showed that an earth sheltered house costing up to 28 percent more initially was still as much as 20 percent cheaper over the life of a thirty-year mortgage. When interest rates are nearly double that earlier level, the implication is unavoidable: if you have to borrow more because your earth sheltered house is more expensive to build, the high interest costs for the additional amount may increase your monthly mortgage pay-

ment enough to outweigh the savings in monthly energy cost.

As a potential owner, weigh the factors of cost against your budget, your design choices, and your energy goals. You may be willing, for example, to trade higher mortgage dollars for lower energy dollars, and therefore would entertain a design that will cost somewhat more to build. If your goal is to reduce the total costs, then make sure that the earth sheltered design you choose will not be more expensive than another energy-efficient alternative.

Visiting Earth Sheltered Homes

There is no substitute for the kind of evaluation possible from firsthand viewing. You will gain further insight concerning what to look for in an earth sheltered home as you read through this book; the final chapter, *Assessing an Existing Earth Sheltered Home*, offers specific suggestions. To find some houses to tour, try the following:

Local resources

- Realtors' knowledge of possible model homes for public view
- Your state society of the American Institute of Architects
- Your state energy office
- A local concrete supplier
- An architecture or engineering school at your state university

National resources (see Appendix B)

- American Underground-Space Association
- Underground Space Center, University of Minnesota
- Center for Natural Energy Design, Oklahoma State University

Chapter 2

Earth Sheltering Defined

To manage an earth sheltered building project intelligently, you must acquire a working familiarity with the terminology, the rationale, and the characteristic features of earth sheltered housing. A basic understanding of how and when earth sheltering works or does not work will be your most important management tool.

Rationale

Earth sheltering is a building concept whose goal is to reduce a structure's exposure to the elements by placing part or all of its walls and roof in direct contact with earth. The actual percentage of surface area that must be covered before a building can be called earth sheltered has never been specifically defined. For purposes of clarity in this book, we will define an earth sheltered house as one with at least a third of its exterior (including both roof and walls) shielded by earth.

What we now consider earth sheltering was born in the late 1960s out of the same general conservation ethic that produced the Environmental Protection Agency. After the 1973 oil embargo, the energy-conserving aspects of earth sheltered design came to the fore. Recognition of earth sheltering as an appropriate solution to the energy problem was expressed most succinctly by a Minnesota banker: "We may not have energy to spare, but we have lots of earth."

The fundamental attraction of earth sheltering is suggested by that remark. Whereas it is appropriate to save scarce energy, it is not only appropriate but satisfying to resolve that scarcity by making use of something that is plentiful and immediately available. Using the structure itself and resources as basic and available as sun and earth, earth sheltering saves energy by responding to its climate rather than artificially controlling it.

Heat Transfer

An understanding of how earth sheltering works begins with understanding the principles of heat transfer. The goal of any energy-conserving strategy is to control heat transfer through the exterior shell, or *envelope*, of a building; in other words, to prevent heat loss to the outside when it is cold and minimize heat gain from the outside when it is hot.

Heat transfer is the movement of energy, in the form of heat, between two objects or spaces having a temperature difference. Two principles of heat transfer help to explain how earth sheltering works. First, the *direction* of heat movement is always from the higher to the lower temperature. Cold, being the absence of heat, does not "move." Second, heat's *rate* of movement is proportional to the difference between the inside and outside temperatures; that is, heat moves faster when it is very hot inside and very cold outside, and vice versa. It moves more slowly when the heat differential between two spaces is smaller.

Several strategies are available to keep heat from leaving or entering a building. Heavily insulating a structure, for example, controls heat transfer by resisting it. Insulation acts like a blanket, impeding the progress of heat to and from the surrounding environment. Earth sheltering, on the other hand, alters the surroundings. Temperatures below ground are consistently more moderate than those above the ground. An earth sheltered building therefore exchanges an environment of frequently uncomfortable air temperatures for the more moderate temperatures of the earth.

Instead of wrapping a blanket around the building, then, earth sheltering is more like moving the building to a moderate climate. Narrowing the difference between the temperature inside and outside the building's envelope actually slows the rate of heat movement.

When the difference in temperature is less and the consequent heat loss or gain is slower, it follows that less energy is needed to keep the inside comfortable. In a cold New York winter, for example, raising the indoor temperature of an above-grade house and sustaining it at a comfortable 68°F means that a difference of perhaps 50° to 70°F between the outside and inside must be maintained if it is very cold outside. On the other hand, as figure 2-2 shows, to keep an earth sheltered house comfortable, you

2–1. Heat moves from a space with a higher temperature to that with a lower temperature.

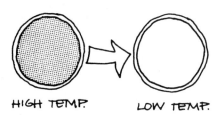

HIGH TEMP.   LOW TEMP.

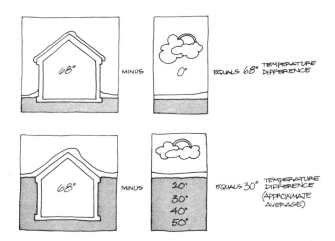

2–2. On a hypothetical 0°F winter day, enough energy to raise the inside temperature by 68°F is required to heat an aboveground house. Below ground, only enough heating energy to raise the temperature an average of 30°F is necessary.

might need to maintain a differential of only 20° to 30°F, because the ground temperature outside the building is already much closer to the comfort level.

Thermal Characteristics of Earth

Earth is, in fact, a fairly good conductor of heat, so you might expect that heat would move away from a warmer, buried structure rather quickly. But earth also has a large heat capacity because of its great mass. The mass responds very slowly to temperature changes.

Below-ground temperatures do eventually reflect seasonal changes above, but so slowly as to lag several months behind (see fig. 2-3). For example, as winter begins, the earth surrounding a house is still holding some of summer's warmth. Conversely, early summer heat is absorbed through earth-covered walls toward the still winter-chilled earth.

The drawings in figure 2-3 demonstrate another thermal characteristic of an earth mass. As the distance down from the ground surface increases, the temperature variations not only lag further behind those at the surface, but also become smaller. At 10 feet down, the ground temperature varies only about 20°F throughout the year, as compared with the much wider range of difference at the surface.

The earth acts, then, as a temperature *moderator*, not as an insulator. In fact, earth is not really very good insulation. It does not resist heat movement as efficiently as manufactured insulation. Rather, its moderating characteristics virtually eliminate the effects of daily air temperature swings on your

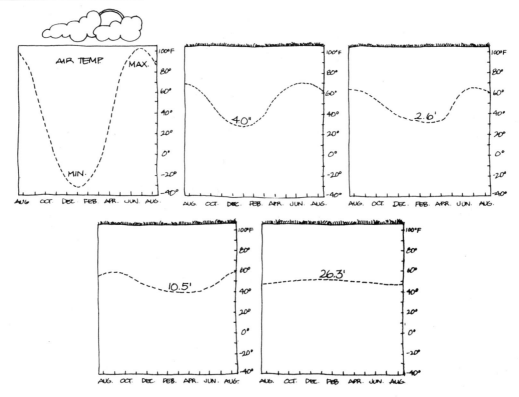

2—3. Air and ground temperatures measured in Minneapolis over the course of a year show that the coldest and warmest temperatures underground occur with increasing delay as the depth increases.

building and even out seasonal temperature fluctuations as well.

Air is not a good conductor of heat. Because air has very little mass, however, its temperature changes fairly quickly. In addition, moving air carries heat along with it. The earth that shelters a building's exterior from the air also functions, therefore, as a *protector*. It protects by reducing heat loss or gain from infiltration (leakages through tiny openings in the shell) and by diminishing or eliminating the effects of cold wind, which carries away a great deal of heat when it washes across a building's surface. If the outside surface is thus made colder, the wider difference in temperature between it and the inside surfaces of the walls increases the rate of heat loss.

Capacity for Free Energy Use

In addition to saving energy, earth covering provides excellent conditions for using free energy from other sources. The moderating effect of the earth mass, when combined with the heat storage potential of masonry building materials, creates ideal conditions for storing intermittent additions of extra heat from both internal sources and from the sun.

Some internal sources of extra heat, a wood-burning stove or fireplace, for example, are intentional. Others coincidentally provide heat as a by-product of their primary use: the refrigerator, dryer, oven, lights — even the inhabitants. When so little heat is being lost to the outside, these sources take on more significance.

If the house is designed properly, an even greater contribution of warmth can come from the sun. Excess heat gained from sunlight entering through windows can be absorbed by masonry, stored there, and then used later. More about this phenomenon, called passive solar heating, will appear later in this chapter.

Aboveground structures can benefit from many of these natural advantages when their backs face cold winter winds and they open to the south for added warmth from the sun. Earth cover and masonry construction offer a wider range of advantages, though, because of the peculiar thermal characteristics of subsurface conditions.

The rationale that explains the dynamics of earth sheltering also suggests the inherent reasons for its attraction. There is satisfaction in saving energy by using resources available on the building site and

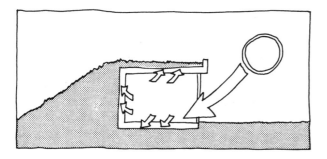

2—4. Masonry functions as temporary storage for excess heat absorbed as direct or reflected sunlight strikes its surface. Stored heat is transferred back to the space when the air in the space becomes cooler than the wall.

by working with natural systems rather than in isolation from them. The pleasure is enhanced by the realization that the systems work passively. When the windows of a house collect solar energy and the floor, walls, and surrounding earth store and protect it, then the house itself *is* the energy system.

What Earth Sheltered Houses Look Like

As the definition given earlier suggests, earth sheltering is a concept involving the substitution of a friendlier climate (the more moderate temperatures of the subsurface) for less friendly aboveground climates. The expression of the concept is not limited to one particular kind of design. A good earth sheltered design should, in fact, respond individually to its own complex of climate, site, and human conditions. To a greater degree than with abovegrade houses, these conditions both challenge and direct the designer's imagination.

In other words, earth sheltered houses do not all look alike. Designs admittedly tend to fall into several generic categories, but to suggest that a design *must* fit such patterns to be successful would be too limiting. Patterns would be in danger of becoming

straitjackets if they are considered the only standards for measuring good design.

Understanding what the typical categories of earth sheltered design are, however, will provide a potential owner with a useful vocabulary. There are three general types of earth sheltered house designs: the elevational plan, the atrium plan, and the penetrational plan.

Elevational Plan

An elevation is one face of a building, seen from the outside. The typical elevational plan exposes one whole face and provides for earth contact on those remaining.

Exterior: The rationale for the elevational approach is that all of the windows can be concentrated on the single exposed wall, allowing all the other exterior surfaces to be covered with earth. The resulting shape is usually long and narrow, since the rooms tend to line up in a row for access to light and the outside. Innovative exterior design is an important consideration for elevational earth sheltered homes: their long, narrow shape requires careful treatment to prevent them from looking like so many railroad cars.

Two-story elevational buildings are often more compact and energy efficient than their single-story counterparts. Multistory buildings in general are potentially more energy efficient than are single-story buildings enclosing the same amount of space, since they usually expose less surface area per cubic foot of volume enclosed.

2—5. Schematic drawing of an elevational plan.

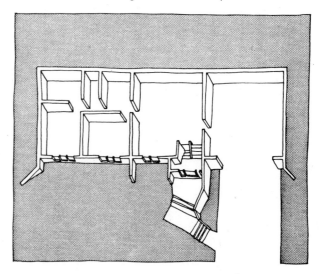

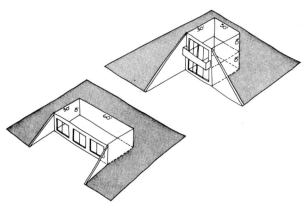

2—6. Both the floor areas and the volumes of these two building shapes are equal. The two-story shape has only 3,720 square feet of surface area, however; the single story has 5,040 square feet, making it less energy efficient (and more costly to build).

2—7. The elevational house at grade level.

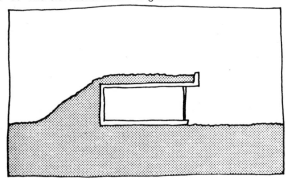

2—8. A semirecessed elevational house.

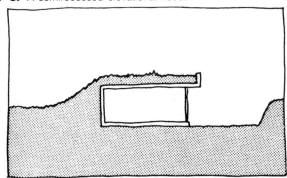

2—9. A fully recessed elevational house.

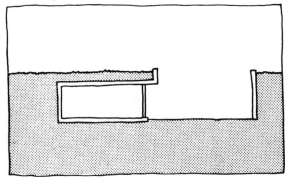

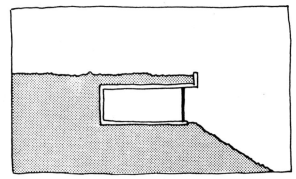

2—10. An elevational house at top of a slope.

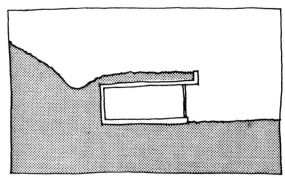

2—11. An elevational house at bottom of a slope.

The elevational structure can be placed at varying depths below the ground surface; it can also be built at grade level.

Interior: Light, views, ventilation, and access are generally available from only one direction in the elevational plan. As in an apartment or a house oriented to a spectacular view, the arrangement of rooms is governed principally by their relative need for windows.

Interior arrangements may present problems to the designer of an elevational house. Hallways can become very long, using valuable space. The organization of adjacent rooms for efficiency, privacy, or communication requires resourcefulness. Entering the house may invite comparisons to entering a cellar if an immediate descent is used; transition between above- and below-ground spaces must be carefully considered.

Figures 2-12 to 2-18 are examples of the range of architectural responses to the exterior and interior limitations of the elevational approach. They demonstrate the extent to which limitations can be translated into opportunities by the architect's imagination and skill.

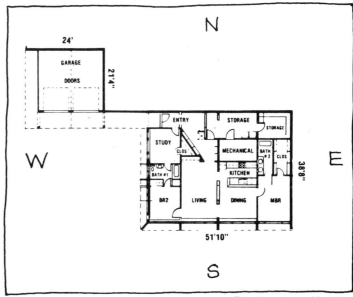

(Floor plan courtesy of Don Metz)

2–12. The "Earthtech 6" floor plan. The open south and west sides allow sunlight and access to the habitable spaces, and the storage, bathroom, and mechanical areas are back in the fully earth sheltered northeast corner.

2–13. "Earthtech 6" is an elevational plan whose design grows out of the work of architect Don Metz of Lyme, NH. Construction drawings for this plan can be purchased (see Appendix B).

(Photo courtesy of Don Metz)

(Photo courtesy of David Scott)

2—14. A park ranger residence in Washington, designed by Professor David M. Scott, FAIA, of Washington State University, was built as a demonstration house as well as a residence. From a distance this elevational house becomes a part of the slope in which it is placed. A more complete description of this entry in AUA's 1981 Design Competition is in *Earth Sheltering: The Form of Energy and the Energy of Form.*

2–15. View of the house from the west, across the newly planted garden and shade trees.

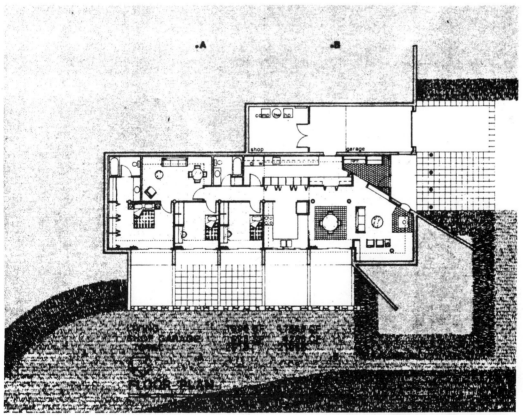

2–16. Floor plan of the ranger residence, showing that the southwest and part of the southeast elevations are opened for light, view, and access.

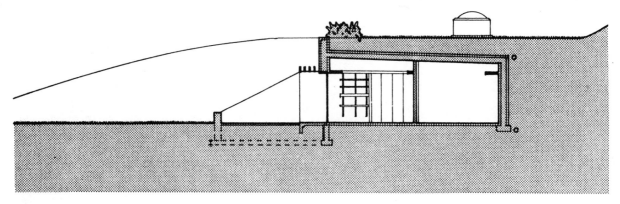

SECTION A•A

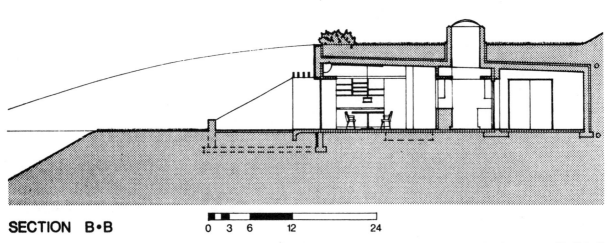

SECTION B•B

0   3   6   12   24

2—17. The ranger residence: cross-sections through the house and through the house and garage.

(Drawings courtesy of David Scott)

2—18. The ranger residence: the front entry (southeast side) is at grade level; the visitor need not step down into the house.

(Photo courtesy of David Scott)

Atrium Plan

An atrium is an internal courtyard. The typical atrium plan features a house that completely or partially surrounds such a courtyard. There are exposed walls in an atrium plan, but they generally face into the courtyard; the other walls are covered with earth.

Exterior: Of the three general earth sheltered plans, the atrium house is least visible from any outside perspective, since its exposed walls are focused inward and the others are buried. Thus the actual shape of the building is usually not discernible from outside. Whether visible or not, however, there is more exposed wall area per unit of volume in an atrium design. The hole in the middle of the house makes it less compact than the others.

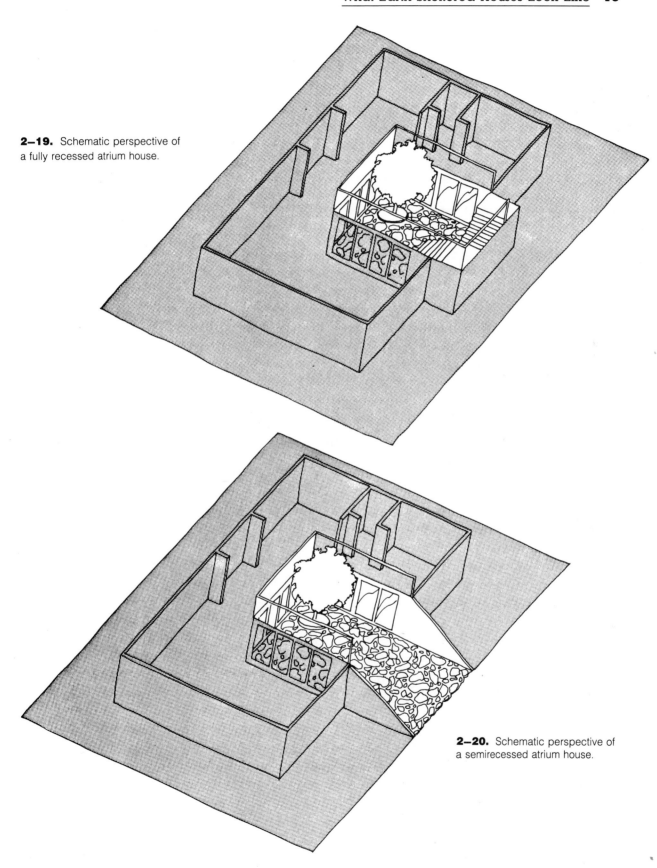

2—19. Schematic perspective of a fully recessed atrium house.

2—20. Schematic perspective of a semirecessed atrium house.

In general, the atrium design is placed more deeply in the earth than the elevational design, though variations often occur when the courtyard is not completely surrounded.

The energy benefit from the atrium plan is generally less than from an elevational plan. In harsh climates an atrium allows undesirable heat transfer through the exposed courtyard walls. Although the window area on these walls may be as great as that of a single exposed wall, less glass can be oriented toward the sun to provide extra heat in a cold climate. In a hot climate, the atrium could trap hot air. In more moderate climates, however, the atrium plan can work very well.

Interior: The atrium house's chief design opportunities—and problems—are modified by its relationship to an open space that is neither wholly outside nor inside. In most climates, for example, walking from one room to another through the atrium is not comfortable in every season. Covering the space solves this problem, as do internal corridors surrounding an open atrium, but both solutions present possible building code problems related to safe fire exits (discussed in the next chapter).

Interior spaces can be arranged quite flexibly in relation to the exposed courtyard-facing walls. Inside visual opportunities are provided by the corners turned and by the atrium space itself. If the entryway is through the courtyard, the transition between outdoors and indoors can be gradual.

Penetrational Plan

A penetration is an opening or interruption in the exterior skin of a building: windows and doors are examples of such openings. A typical penetrational plan interrupts the earth covering the walls, opening up windows or doorways to the outside by holding back the earth on either side of them.

Exterior: The penetrational approach enables windows and entry points to occur on more than one

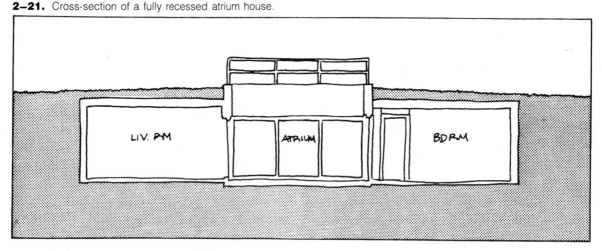

2–21. Cross-section of a fully recessed atrium house.

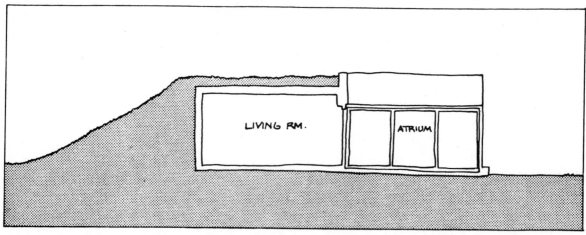

2–22. Cross-section of a semirecessed atrium house.

2–23. The glass-covered atrium in a house that Massachusetts architect John E. Barnard, Jr., adapted from among his several standard plans. Two of the home's three bedrooms and the living room have sliding glass doors opening into the atrium.

(Photo courtesy of John Barnard, Jr.; reprinted with permission of photographer, Phokion Karas, Medford, MA)

face of a building. Rather than alter the interior arrangements, the earth-cover configuration itself is altered to accommodate needs for light or views, access to the outside, and cross-ventilation.

The shape of a penetrational plan is likely to be the most compact of all three approaches. From the outside the house may appear complicated and sprawling, however, because holding the earth back from the openings usually requires retaining walls:

upright, sloping, or stepped walls radiating outward from the building face.

The penetrational house is rarely built very deeply into the ground, since excavating down to a window level would make no sense. Many such houses are built on grade, and the earth is piled up, or bermed, around the structure.

Making the penetrational design both energy efficient and cost-effective requires careful attention

2–24. Tedd F. Chilless, AIA, of Chilless Nielsen Architects in Portland, OR, designed this atrium plan house for himself. He describes a "pleasant excitement living in the space and it is all due to being earth sheltered."

(Photo courtesy of Tedd Chilless)

(Photo courtesy of Tedd Chilless)

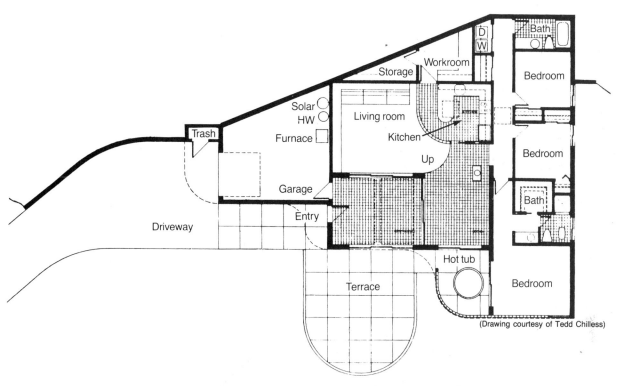

(Drawing courtesy of Tedd Chilless)

2—26. Floor plan of the Chilless house.

2—25. At left. Interior view of Chilless house from the covered atrium.

2—27. The use of sliding glass doors and interior partitions of glass block allow rooms to borrow light from each other and from the atrium.

(Photo courtesy of Tedd Chilless)

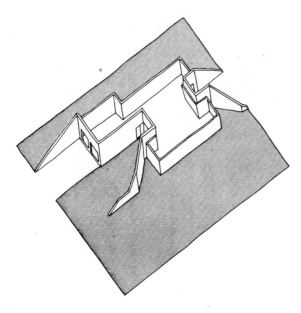

2—28. Schematic drawing of a penetrational house *without* roof or any earth covering. Only the retaining walls and the front and rear elevations would be visible if the earth cover were present (see fig. 2—29).

2—29. Schematic drawing of a penetrational house *with* its earth covering. Except at the openings for doors and windows, earth is piled up and over the structure.

to both the placement and the frequency of openings in the earth cover. Interruptions reduce earth's effectiveness as a moderator and storage mass, and they offer more opportunity for infiltration. Retaining walls can be expensive to construct, especially if they are high. Further, they will draw, or *wick*, heat out of a building unless an insulated break (called a *thermal break*) is provided between them and the building shell.

Interior: Choices for room arrangements and internal circulation in the penetrational approach are nearly the same as in a conventional aboveground structure. In fact, a strict penetrational design resembles an aboveground house with earth and retaining walls added.

Survey of House Plans

Study some books of plans and designs. It is too soon to order any specific plans; you should have a site in mind when and if you decide to purchase standard plans. Looking at the range of plans and building systems available from earth sheltered builders will, however, teach you a good deal about the state of the commercial art, and the houses and plans described in the publications below will bring you up to date concerning what architecture has to offer (see Appendix A for details).

- *Earth Sheltered Homes: Plans and Designs*, Underground Space Center
- *Underground Designs*, Malcolm Wells
- *Underground Plans Book—1*, Malcolm Wells and Sam Glenn-Wells
- *Earth Sheltering: The Form of Energy and the Energy of Form*, T. Lance Holthusen and Ed Frenette
- Predesigned plan books from designers or builders, listed in Appendix C

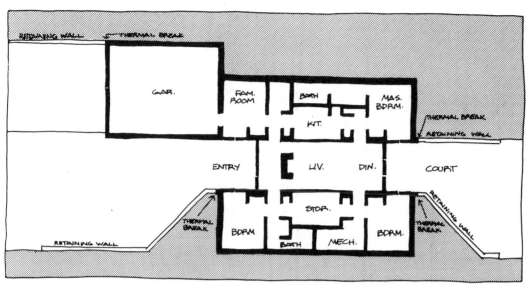

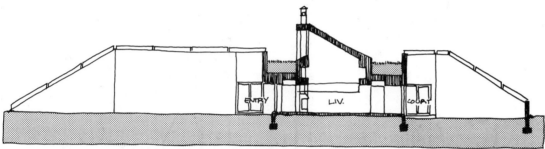

2—30. The Design Consortium Inc., a Minneapolis architecture firm, has combined a covered atrium (the central living-dining area) with elements of the penetrational house. Circulation, fire safety exiting, and daylighting problems have been solved resourcefully, and the number of penetrations has been kept to a minimum.

(Photo courtesy of Design Consortium Inc.)

2—31. The south elevation of the Design Consortium house, which was designed and built as part of a demonstration project of the Minnesota Housing Finance Agency. This house and the others in the demonstration project are illustrated in the Underground Space Center's book, *Earth Sheltered Homes: Plans and Designs*.

The Specific Anatomy of Earth Sheltered Houses

An efficient close-up description necessarily concentrates on the points of difference between earth sheltered and conventional houses; the result inevitably suggests that the differences outweigh the similarities. From the outside the differences are more evident. On the inside an earth sheltered house looks and feels, to the surprise of many, very similar to a conventional house.

In this section only features that differ are highlighted: building materials, waterproofing, insulation, lighting, ventilation, and energy systems. You will need to have a working knowledge of these anatomical features when assessing a design and also when observing construction. More detailed information about their characteristics is given in chapter 9.

Structural Materials

The choice of structural material for an earth sheltered house is governed by a range of demands. To work well below grade, it needs to be quite strong, durable, and provide both a very tight enclosure and a good surface for waterproofing and insulation. Materials should be available nearby to reduce transportation costs and may additionally be expected to provide mass for storing heat from the sun.

The material that answers most of these needs is concrete. As compared with wood, the possible disadvantages of concrete are that residential con-

2–32. Concrete that is poured, rather than precast and cured at the factory, is called cast-in-place concrete. It arrives at the building site in the rotating body of the familiar concrete truck.

tractors are less familiar with its use, and its heavy weight requires larger footings.

Concrete structural materials come in varying shapes and forms: concrete is either poured at the building site or precast into panels, planks, or blocks at the factory and then assembled at the site.

Although not as massive as concrete, wood offers some advantages and is used in some earth sheltered houses. Its lighter weight makes it easier to handle, and home builders are much more experienced in wood construction. As in any wood foundation, however, the portions of a wood structural system that come in contact with earth must be treated with a chemical preservative to prevent decomposition.

Large steel culverts offer intriguing possibilities for earth sheltering because they are strong and watertight and their curved shapes can be pleasing. Few homes have actually been built using culverts, possibly because of potential problems associated with fire and corrosion protection and because of the structural problems associated with designs calling for many openings in the shell.

2–34. Schematic drawing of a house in River Falls, WI, showing how steel culverts were used in the design.

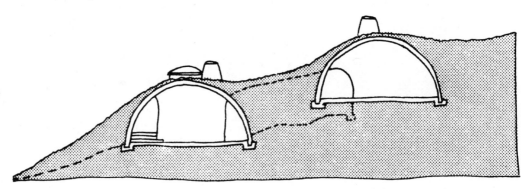

Waterproofing

Waterproofing failure is one of the greatest fears in earth sheltered construction, with good reason. Leaks are harder to find and costlier to repair than they are in an above-grade house. The earth sheltered owner should be wary of the miracle product or the simple solution.

Materials that are chosen and applied in tried-and-true waterproofing aboveground, like asphalt or pitch, may not be dependable below ground. In fact, the choice of material for the waterproof skin on the building's exterior surface is only the last line of defense against leaks. Herein lies the chief difference in earth sheltering's approach to waterproofing; it is much more comprehensive. The successful waterproofing system will first include a good landscape and drainage plan, a building design that limits the number of areas particularly susceptible to leaks, and protection for the sometimes delicate watertight materials. In many instances this protection can be provided by the insulation.

Insulation

In contrast to above-grade houses, on which insulation is applied just inside the exterior sheathing, insulation is usually placed on the outside of earth sheltered walls. The temperature stability provided by massive building materials is thus not isolated from the interior spaces. Furthermore, exterior insulation can double as a protective covering for the waterproofing by being placed outside of the waterproof skin as well.

Because insulation placed outside both the shell and the waterproofing comes in contact with the earth and its moisture, a product must be chosen

2—33. An all-wood house in Redwood Falls, MN, designed and built by Everstrong Marketing, Inc., and used as a model home.

(Photo courtesy of Everstrong Marketing, Inc.)

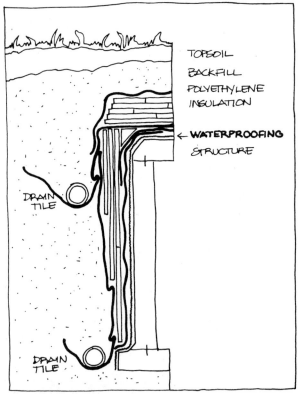

TOPSOIL
BACKFILL
POLYETHYLENE
INSULATION
← **WATERPROOFING**
STRUCTURE

DRAIN TILE

DRAIN TILE

(From "*Earth Sheltered Structures Fact Sheets, #4,* "Waterproofing Considerations and Materials")

2—35. Section detail of a wall, showing schematic drainage, backfill, waterproofing, and insulation elements.

that does not absorb moisture and thereby lose its effectiveness. Rigid insulation boards of certain kinds are more characteristic of earth sheltering than the fiberglass bats commonly used for interior insulation above grade.

Lighting and Ventilation

In above-grade houses windows and entries perform a triple function: they provide light and ventilation, as well as access to the outside. With fewer opportunities for doors and accessible windows on all sides, the earth sheltered house designer must often separate these functions.

Various options are available for additional lighting. Artificial lighting is the most accessible solution, but excessive need for it in the daytime contradicts the assumed energy-saving intent of an earth sheltered project. Skylights or other high windows and borrowed light from adjacent rooms are frequently good solutions for bringing in light to more remote portions of the interior.

Most aboveground houses leak enough air to make artificial means of exchanging inside and outside air unnecessary. In a tightly sealed earth sheltered house with openings concentrated on one or two sides, however, air exchange and circulation require more attention.

Good ventilation and energy conservation are in some respects contradictory goals. On the one hand, the aim is to introduce and circulate outside air to remove moisture, odors, and indoor air pollutants; on the other, the aim is to prevent outside air from bringing unwanted chill or heat inside. Air brought in intentionally we call ventilation; what enters by accident is infiltration.

2—36. Ways to bring daylight into the house

SKYLIGHT:

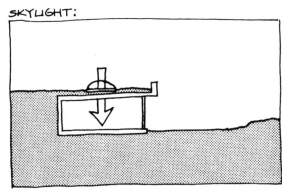

CLERESTORY WINDOW:

RAISED ROOF ANGLES:

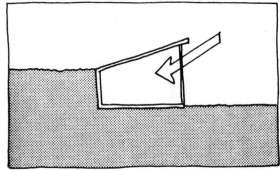

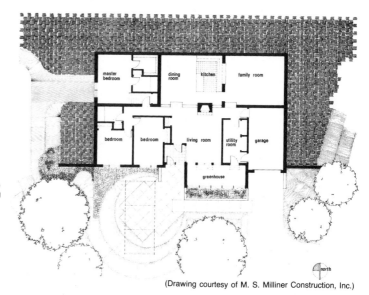

2—37. Floor plan of the 2,300–square foot Milliner house, illustrating the open living area's ability to share light from living room to dining area and kitchen.

(Drawing courtesy of M. S. Milliner Construction, Inc.)

2—38. Clerestory windows above and a greenhouse in front bring light into both back and front of this Maryland house by M. S. Milliner Construction, Inc., Frederick, MD.

(Photo courtesy of M. S. Milliner Construction, Inc.)

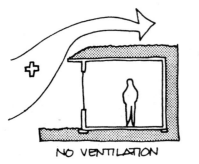

NO VENTILATION

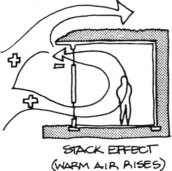

STACK EFFECT
(WARM AIR RISES)

ROOF PENETRATION
PROVIDES NEGATIVE PRESSURE

2–39. Ways to induce natural ventilation. (From *Earth Sheltered Structures Fact Sheets*, #8, "Indoor Air Quality")

Natural ventilation, therefore, is good when the air coming in does not defeat heating or cooling needs by being the wrong temperature. A flow of air can be created by arranging the windows, doors, and vents or chimneys to take advantage of natural convection and prevailing winds. In most climates, however, supplemental mechanical systems, such as exhaust fans, are necessary for ventilation.

Active and Passive Solar Design

Earth sheltering is a conservation strategy; its purpose is to reduce the amount of energy needed to heat and cool. The goal of a solar system, on the other hand, is to add energy by converting sunlight directly into warmth that can be used to heat spaces and/or water. Active and particularly passive solar systems are so compatible with earth sheltering that understanding how they work is necessary in order to comprehend the full possibilities of earth sheltered buildings.

Solar heating systems have three common functional components: collection, storage, and distribution of heat. The difference between active and passive solar systems lies principally in how heat is distributed. An active system uses "active" mechanical devices such as pumps or fans to force the movement of heat from the collection point to where it will be either stored or used. The passive system relies on the natural properties of heat for distribution.

The collection and storage strategies for active and passive systems often differ as well. An active system features separate panels for collecting solar radiation. In a passive system, the openings for solar collection are windows; one is, in a sense, living in the collector. An active system relies on such nonstructural materials as rocks or water for storing the heat collected by the panels; in a passive system the walls, ceiling, and floors of a building often serve as storage for the heat.

Active Systems

Even though earth sheltering reduces the size requirements for an active system, particularly with regard to the amount of separate storage necessary, an active system involves a larger front-end investment than does a passive system. This is because, unlike passive solar systems, active systems are not designed as part of the house structure; rather, they are additional features that serve only the single purpose of converting solar energy into heat. In addition, the equipment used to collect, store, and distribute heat is more complex and therefore more susceptible to breakdown. For these reasons active systems are not used very frequently for residential space heating. They appear to be more appropriate in larger buildings when penetration of direct light into the space is undesirable.

Heating (or preheating) domestic water with active solar, however, is another story. With lower space heating needs, water heating could reflect the largest part of an earth sheltered home owner's utility bill. Since payback periods for active solar water heating systems can be as low as five years, such an investment appears to be sensible.

Passive Systems

To understand passive solar heating, you must first understand what it is not. It is "inactive" in the sense that warmth is not moved artificially by special mechanical pumps or fans from an outside collection point, through a storage area, and then into a living space. A passive system is rather an opportunistic one; it uses natural, unforced means of heat transfer and commonly takes advantage of building components already inherent in the structure to convert solar radiation into useful heat.

A passive system works somewhat like a closed car in the sun. Sunlight entering the car through its glass is absorbed by dark surfaces. When the radiation is thus converted from short-wave to long-wave radiation, it cannot escape through the glass, and the interior therefore heats up. Passively heated spaces work like enlarged cars; the windows allow radiation to enter, dark surfaces on floors or walls absorb the radiation, and the space is warmed.

Good passive solar design can double the efficiency of an earth sheltered house. Its contribution of heat, in other words, can reduce net heating energy use in a building by half. The extra front-end cost need not be great; since thermal storage is probably already present in a masonry structure anyway, the biggest additional investment will be in correct design.

Like earth sheltering itself, however, passive solar is a deceptively simple idea. A hit-or-miss system ("put the windows on the south and add some thermal storage") will provide some savings. A closer look at how passive collection, storage, and distribution actually function will demonstrate, however, that a successful passive system depends on informed and quite sophisticated design choices.

Collection: Collection of the optimum amount of solar radiation depends upon the type, size, orientation, and tilt of the windows. In cold climates, for example, the type of collecting window chosen must feature some insulation if gains during the day are to exceed losses back through the glass at night. Double or triple glazed windows or glass block are types of windows that offer better insulation than single panes of glass, but each additional layer of glass will also reduce somewhat the transmission of solar radiation. Additional insulation applied at night further reduces nighttime losses.

An area of night-insulated south-facing windows equal to 25 to 50 percent of the room's floor area will produce a healthy net solar gain, assuming the storage, distribution, and building insulation are

2—40. Schematic active solar system with forced air distribution.

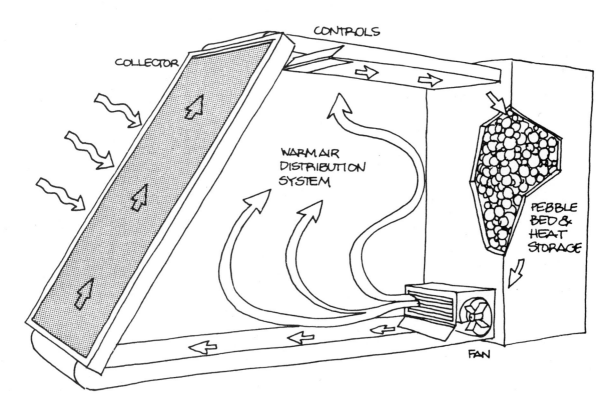

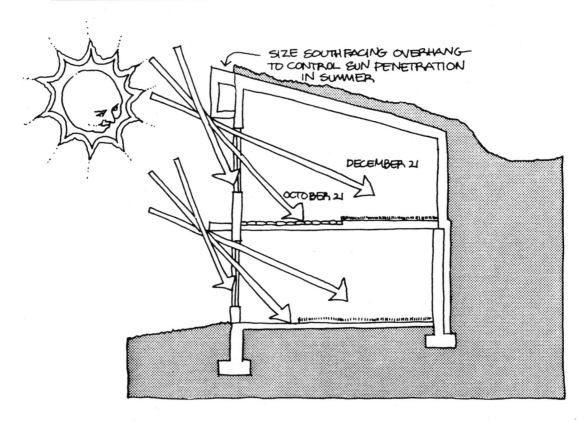

2—41. Proper shading eliminates unwanted summer sun while allowing deep penetration of sunlight in winter. Dark tile or brick absorbs radiation; the concrete floor beneath stores it. Carpet prevents absorption, thereby rendering the storage useless.

correct. Although the south orientation is normally the best, windows facing up to 30 degrees east or west of south are acceptable; their orientation affects the time of day when the sunlight entering the house will be most intense (east windows allow more intense sunlight to enter in the morning; west windows, in the afternoon).

The tilt is sensitive to seasonal variations in sun height. With no tilt at all, an ordinary vertical window on a wall takes in low-altitude winter sun. More horizontal glass, for example, on a sloped roof, takes in more summer sunlight. It is for this reason that the collector panel for an active solar hot water system, which must capture sunlight year-round, generally tilts more than the upright collector window used primarily for winter heating that can be shaded from the higher summer sun.

Storage: Thermal storage is perhaps the most critical part of the passive system, and the least understood. Without some storage mass, either water or massive building materials like concrete and brick, the contribution of heat will be uncontrolled, the space will

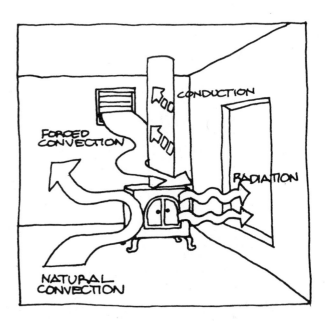

2—42. The three methods of heat transfer, radiation, convection, and conduction, are used in various combinations to distribute heat in the common types of passive solar systems illustrated in figures 2–43, 2–44, and 2–45.

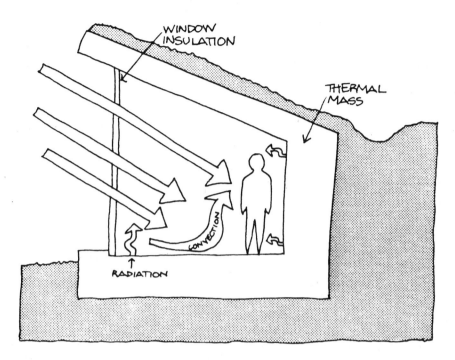

WINDOW
INSULATION

THERMAL
MASS

CONVECTION

RADIATION

2–43. A *direct gain system* is probably the simplest passive system for an earth sheltered house. Sunlight enters the space through south-facing glass, is converted to heat at the absorbing surfaces, and is distributed throughout the space by convection and radiation.

2–44. An *attached sunspace* can be both a collector and a greenhouse. Thermal storage is placed between the sunspace and the living space to be heated, using radiation, convection, and conduction to distribute the heat. The sunspace can be isolated so that its temperature can drop at night without cooling the living space.

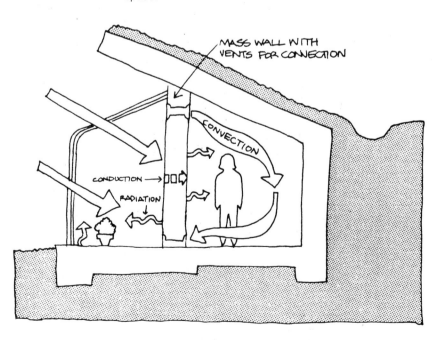

MASS WALL WITH
VENTS FOR CONVECTION

CONVECTION

CONDUCTION →

RADIATION

WATER WALL SYSTEM:

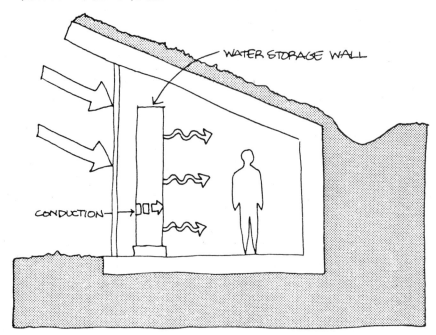

WATER STORAGE WALL

CONDUCTION

TROMBE WALL SYSTEM:

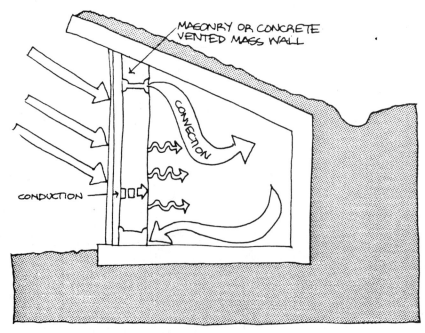

MASONRY OR CONCRETE VENTED MASS WALL

CONVECTION

CONDUCTION

2—45. A *mass wall system* locates vertical thermal mass directly inside the window. The mass wall can either be vented (allowing convection as well as conduction) or unvented (transfer by con- duction only). A mass wall of solid masonry or concrete is called a Trombe (pronounced *trahm*) wall, after its inventor. Mass walls of water stored in containers are also fairly common.

overheat, and this excess heat will likely be vented back outside by uncomfortable occupants. After sunset a building without mass will cool quickly.

The function of thermal storage mass is to absorb heat when it is in excess and release it later to heat the space when room temperatures drop. Primary thermal mass (in direct sun from 10:00 AM to 2:00 PM)is four times as effective as mass receiving only reflected light. The appropriate material, location, amount, and thickness of the storage mass are all important factors in the proper functioning of the whole system.

Distribution: Transferring heat around a living space in a passive system is, by definition, accomplished by natural means. The three modes of heat transfer that come into play are radiation, convection, and conduction. Perhaps the simplest way to describe the three is to use the example of a stove.

Radiation of heat from the stove warms adjacent surfaces; heat radiated from the surface travels in the form of electromagnetic waves without warming the medium (air) through which it moves. In fact, if the radiant temperature of your own surroundings is at or slightly above your skin temperature, you feel comfortable even though the air temperature may be lower than what is normally considered comfortable. *Convection* is the transfer of heat by its carrier's movement; that is, by the rising of air that is warmed by passing over the stove's warm surface. *Conduction*, which transfers heat by direct molecular action through a medium, moves warmth from the firebox to other parts of the stove itself. Another example of conduction is the heating of the handle

of a pot whose bottom is being heated on the stove.

Three of the most common types of passive solar designs are illustrated in figures 2-43, 2-44, and 2-45. They are distinguished from one another primarily by the location of the thermal storage.

Further Reading

Read and learn as much as you can about earth sheltering. Several organizations do research and share information: the Underground Space Center at the University of Minnesota, the American Underground-Space Association (AUA), and the Center for Natural Energy Design at Oklahoma State University. Contact them for suggested reading lists and publications catalogs (addresses are in Appendix B).

An alternative to earth sheltering that is aboveground but saves equivalent amounts of energy is the *superinsulated* house. With large amounts of insulation and extremely careful control of infiltration and conduction heat loss, this technique is also worth some investigation.

From "Further Reading" in Appendix A we recommend:

● *Earth Sheltered Housing Design: Guidelines, Examples and References*, Underground Space Center, University of Minnesota
● *Earth Sheltered Structures: Fact Sheet Series*, prepared by the Underground Space Center and the Center for Natural Energy Design for the U.S. Department of Energy
● *Earth Shelter Living* (bimonthly periodical)
● *The Passive Solar Energy Book*, Edward Mazria
● *Super Insulated Homes and Double Envelope Houses*, William A. Shurcliff

Chapter 3

Climate and Location

This chapter and the next are designed to provide criteria for selecting a suitable site if you do not yet own one. They will also suggest ways to gather, evaluate, and organize the predesign information embodied in a site description.

Site information makes up the first part of what architects call a *program* for a house. A program is not a design, but rather a written set of directions and space requirements that will help to determine the design. Composing a program is a good way to organize both site research and personal analysis. The resulting document will communicate concisely and clearly the information that your designer needs to fit the house both to you and to your site.

To help you organize the process of evaluating, selecting, and describing a site, we will begin with regional considerations, work down through locational factors, then specific site factors, and finally arrive at suggestions for selecting and purchasing a lot. By finding and recording your particular information at each level, you will gradually accumulate the raw material to produce a site map, the vehicle for the site-descriptive part of your program.

Region

Regional Climates and Earth Sheltered Design

In general, earth sheltering can save energy in any region of the country. Recent research has shown, however, that earth sheltering for energy saving is more cost-effective in some regions than in others and that the optimum amount of earth cover for energy economy also varies from region to region.

Discovering the relative suitability of earth sheltering to regional climates presents a complex problem. To solve it, analytical studies for the Navy Facilities Engineering Command were performed by Setter, Leach & Lindstrom Inc., a Minneapolis architectural, engineering, and planning firm, and their consultant, the Underground Space Center of the University of Minnesota. They considered both climate and building design factors.

The navy research suggests that four interrelated climate characteristics must be considered in evaluating earth sheltering's usefulness in your region.

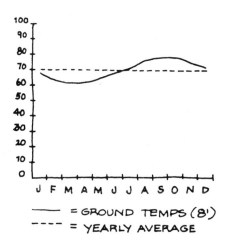

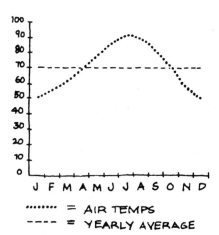

3—1. Though the daily temperatures over the course of a year fluctuate more widely aboveground, the yearly temperature *averages* above and below the surface, shown with the horizontal dashed lines in each graph, are nearly the same.

(Data for Phoenix, AZ, is taken from tables prepared by Kenneth Labs in *A Regional Analysis of Ground and Above Ground Climate*, U.S. Department of Energy)

These factors are ground temperature, air temperature, humidity, and air movement. Since these factors are interrelated, it is cumbersome and misleading to consider each in isolation from the others; they are best discussed in pairs. A fifth factor in determining climate suitability is a design factor: the amount of earth cover on the earth sheltered structure itself will modify the extent to which earth sheltering is suitable in a given climate.

Ground Temperature vs. Air Temperature: The temperature below the surface of the ground in any region, taken all by itself, is not the sole criterion; neither is the temperature of the air alone. Considered separately, these factors will not help you determine your climate's suitability for earth sheltering. Rather, the relationship between the ground temperature and the outside air temperature is the main consideration.

The *average* annual ground temperature of any region is actually roughly equivalent to the *average* of the annual air temperatures. (Several kinds of surface conditions cause exceptions to this statement; for example, snow cover isolates the earth from winter's cold air, so that the average annual ground temperature in snowy regions will be slightly higher than the average annual air temperature.) If you know what your climate's average annual temperature is, then you will also know roughly what the ground temperatures average out to over a year.

In the real world, however, actual temperatures rarely equal the average. Both air and ground temperatures fluctuate with the seasons, though the ground temperature lags behind changes in the air. Therefore, temperature *extremes*, not averages, are what buildings experience. Actual air temperature fluctuations are what we consider when evaluating the ability of the seasonal ground temperature to moderate the extremes.

When we must compare the temperature fluc-

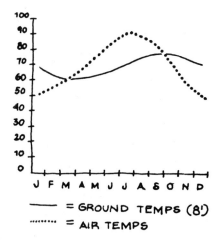

(Data from tables prepared by Kenneth Labs)

3—2. A comparison of the actual temperature *extremes* that would be experienced above and below ground, again in Phoenix, AZ. The earth is twenty degrees warmer in winter and is cooler by the same amount in summer.

tuations in one climate with those of another in order to determine the relative suitability of earth sheltering, a system to quantify the amounts of variation is required. Fortunately, such a system has been developed; it is the concept of *degree days*. Unfortunately, it is initially a difficult concept to grasp.

The number of degree days assigned to a climate or area indicates the temperature variation above and below a comfortable temperature; in other words, degree days indicate an area's heating and cooling requirements. First an arbitrary comfortable temperature is established. When heating requirements are being measured, this point has been established at 65°F. Then the difference in degrees between this point and the average outdoor temperature during one full day (twenty-four hours) is computed. The result becomes the number of degree days assigned to that day.

For example, a winter day and night with an outdoor average of 20°F will result in a measurement of 45 heating degree days (the 65°F base point minus the actual 20°F); an outdoor average of 50°F will equal only 15 heating degree days. When all the twenty-four hour periods in a year are added up, a colder climate will have a higher total of heating degree days, or a higher heating requirement. Fargo, North Dakota, has approximately 9,270 heating degree days over a year; St. Louis has about 4,750.

Cooling degree days are computed similarly but use an arbitrary comfort temperature of 75°F. The number of degrees by which each daily average exceeds 75°F will be totaled for the year to quantify the annual cooling degree days, or the annual cooling requirements. Fargo's cooling degree days are 473; St. Louis has 1,578.

The higher the number of heating and cooling degree days in a given area, the more extreme are the temperatures and the more suitable earth covering is for moderating those extremes. In a climate where air temperatures are moderate and do remain relatively constant over the year, little extra energy benefit is produced by protecting a home from the air with earth.

In warm climates, western Oklahoma and Texas, for example, earth sheltering offers potential for saving energy by reducing the need for air-conditioning. Although the reduction in cooling needs may not equal the reduction in heating needs farther north, cost savings may still be equivalent because air-conditioning uses electricity, generally a more expensive and less efficient source of energy.

Whether your house must respond to hot summers or cold winters, then, it could be said as a general rule that the greater the climate control needs, the more suitable it is to use a design that responds to such needs efficiently. Thus, where both heating and cooling degree days are high, meaning temperatures are more extreme, more benefit is realized from earth sheltering. Such a rule assumes, however, that the ground temperature has the right relationship to those extremes.

What is the right relationship? The perfect relationship would feature a ground climate that is exactly the opposite of the seasonal climate extremes you are sheltering against; that is, cool during the hottest months and warm in the depths of winter.

Of course, such a balance cannot be completely achieved, because ground temperatures do not lag six months behind air temperatures at shallow depths. Nevertheless, the wider the differential between above- and below-ground temperatures, the better the energy saving potential is (see fig. 3-3).

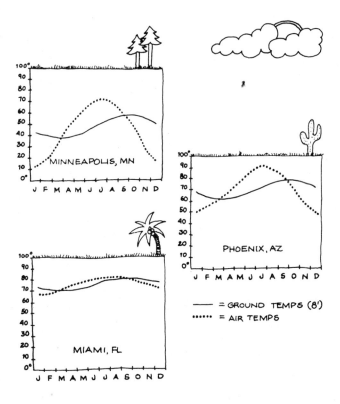

(Data from tables prepared by Kenneth Labs)

3–3. Comparison of air and ground temperature variations (eight feet down) for Minneapolis, Phoenix, and Miami. The wider the difference between air and ground temperatures in any season, the more potential energy benefit would be gained by building underground.

It follows that, given the temperature lag below ground, the greatest differential will be found where the warmest summers alternate with the coldest winters, leaving their successive subsurface imprints behind them for several months.

Air Movement and Humidity: How comfortable you actually feel at a given temperature also depends on another set of interrelated factors: air movement and humidity. For example, even at a comfortable temperature of 68°F, moving air will make you feel cold. High humidity at 68°F, on the other hand, will make you feel too warm. Air movement can mitigate the effects of high humidity.

Designing for a hot climate with high humidity, for example, requires one of two strategies for keeping the inside comfortably cool. The first is to lower the humidity by air-conditioning—there is no well-developed nonmechanical way to remove moisture from air. The second, more energy-efficient alternative is to provide air movement through good natural ventilation.

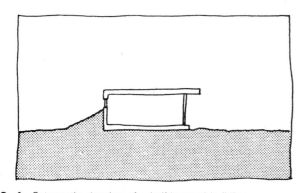

3—4. Schematic drawing of a half-bermed building.

Total earth sheltering however, does not generally provide as much cross-ventilation as above-ground designs do. Furthermore, moist air produces condensation when it comes in contact with a colder surface such as a wall backed by earth. Thus, humid climates are least appropriate for earth sheltering.

In summary, to evaluate a climate for earth sheltering, consider (in progressive order):

- humidity (less is more suitable);
- normal mechanical heating and cooling requirements (more is more suitable);
- ability of ground temperature to counteract the heating and cooling load (greater is more suitable).

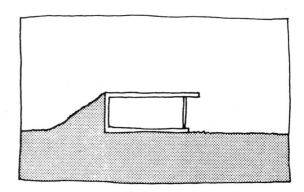

3—5. Schematic drawing of a fully bermed building.

The benefits of earth sheltering increase as a given climate meets the above requirements.

Building Design: The shape of the building and the amount of earth cover will also affect the degree to which an earth sheltered house is a suitably cost-effective strategy for energy conservation in your climate.

In terms of shape, a compact structure with a low ratio of roof area to total volume is more cost-effective to earth shelter. Covering walls with earth is cheaper than covering roofs, and the benefits are greater.

In terms of earth cover, three different configurations must be considered.

Half-Bermed: This is the lowest level of covering. Earth extends perhaps halfway up the walls, leaving room for windows aboveground. Half-berming provides the least energy benefit of the three configurations, though infiltration is reduced and temperatures are moderated somewhat.

If your climate is hot and humid, however, a half-bermed building may still be a better energy solution than a totally exposed building would be. Half-berming will not necessarily interfere with your potential for natural ventilation or solar gain, and the extra cost will be insignificant unless there are multiple openings through the berms. In other words, half-berming could make earth sheltering suitable in climates where it would not normally be considered.

Fully Bermed: Buried up to the tops of the walls but having a conventional roof, this configuration is the optimum level of earth covering for most climates. It does not save the most energy but is nevertheless the most cost-effective of the three alternatives because covering walls brings the most energy savings at the least cost.

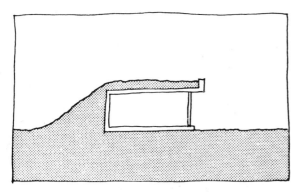

3—6. Schematic drawing of a fully earth sheltered building.

Fully Earth Sheltered: In climates to which earth sheltering is most suited, covering the roof with a maximum of two to three feet of soil is certainly the most energy conserving of the three alternatives. From the sole standpoint of initial cost plus energy use, however, covering the roof is seldom cost-effective.

The weight of the earth on the roof dictates a sturdy structure. The added structural costs for supporting a heavy roof are not adequately balanced by the resulting energy savings. The heating and cooling advantages can be achieved less expensively by other kinds of roof systems with good (and much lighter weight) insulation.

This assertion, coming from the navy research, will be something of a shock to singleminded earth sheltering advocates. Before going directly back to the drawing board, however, stop and consider that energy economy is not always the only reason for earth sheltering. Personal taste and the site itself might suggest other good reasons. If economy *is* your sole aim, however, then do not cover your roof.

Evaluating the Climate Suitability of Your Region

Kenneth Labs, architect and researcher at Undercurrent Design Research in New Haven, Connecticut, has completed considerable research on how the relationship between ground temperature and climate can guide the use of earth tempering strategies. The following map (fig. 3-7) and explanation are taken from his study for the U.S. Department of Energy, *A Regional Analysis of Ground and Above Ground Climate.* The map will help you find the general applicability of earth sheltering to your particular region.

Mr. Labs cautions:

Climate control ordinarily is a very complex problem which defies simple conclusions. This is particularly true of earth sheltering, where the complexities of both above and below ground climate must be evaluated simultaneously. At the risk of oversimplification and possible future misinterpretation, however, it is felt that the major design-related issues of ground versus aboveground climate are most vividly summarized in a single map.

Synopsis of Regional Earth Tempering Issues

A. Ideal Summer and Winter Suitability. Cold, cloudy winters maximize value of earth tempering as a heat conservation measure. Cool soil and dry summers favor subgrade placement and earth covered roofs, with little likelihood of condensation.

B. Excellent Summer and Winter Suitability. Severely cold winters demand major heat conservation measures, even though more sunshine is available here than on the coast. Dry summers and cool soil favor earth-covered roofs and ground coupling.

C. Strong Summer and Winter Benefits. Good winter insulation somewhat lessens the need for extraordinary winter heat conservation, but value of summer benefit is more important here than in the zone above. Earth covering is advantageous, the ground offers some cooling, condensation is no problem, and ventilation is not a major necessity.

D. Major Winter Benefit, Summer Mixed Blessings. Cold and often cloudy winters place a premium on heat conservation. Low summer ground temperatures offer a cooling source but with the likelihood of condensation. High summer humidity makes ventilation the leading summer climate control strategy. An aboveground superinsulated house designed to maximize ventilation is an important competing design approach.

E. Marginal Winter and Summer Benefit. Generally good winter sun and minor heating demand reduce the need for extreme heat conservation measures. The ground offers protection from overheated air, but not major cooling potential as a heat sink. The primacy of ventilation and the possibility of condensation compromise summer benefits. Quality of design will determine actual benefit realized here.

F. Insignificant Winter Benefit, Small or Negative Summer Benefit. High ground temperatures actually increase annual cooling load with reference to base 65°F cooling degree days. Persistent high humidity levels negate value of roof mass and establish ventilation as the only important summer cooling strategy. Any design that compromises ventilation effectiveness

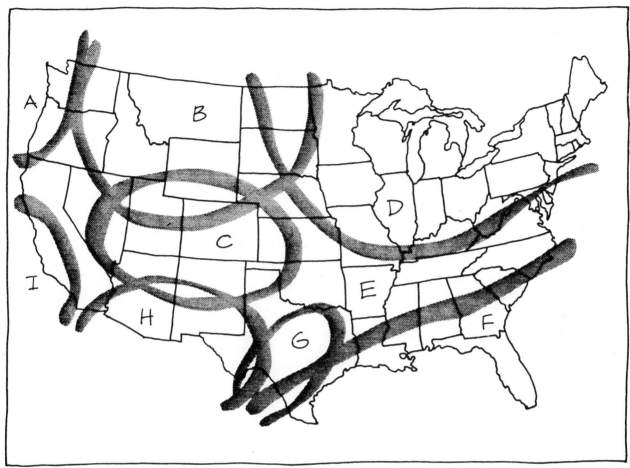

(From Kenneth Labs's *A Regional Analysis of Ground and Above Ground Climate,* prepared for the U.S. Department of Energy)

3—7. "Synopsis of Regional Earth Tempering Issues" shows, very generally, the suitability of earth sheltering to regional climates in the United States.

without contributing to cooling is considered counterproductive.

G. Insignificant Winter Benefit, Marginal Summer Benefit. This is a transition area between zones F and H, comments concerning which apply here in degree. The value of earth tempering increases moving westward through this zone, and diminishes moving southward.

H. Insignificant Winter Benefit, Useful Summer Advantage. Summer ground temperatures are high, but relatively much cooler than air. Aridity favors roof mass, reduces need for ventilation, eliminates concern about condensation. Potential for integrating earth tempering with other passive design alternatives is high.

I. Insignificant to Marginal Winter and Summer Benefit. Extraordinary means of climate control are not required due to relative moderateness of this zone. Earth tempering is compatible with other winter and summer strategies, with no strong argument for or against it.

Labs has a very important last word:

Earth tempering offers benefits on its own terms for most areas of the United States. When compared to the appropriateness of other passive design techniques, however, some of these benefits are outweighed by the potential disadvantages. The real measure of this value cannot be found in analyses of raw data: the climate control successfulness of any structure ultimately depends not upon whether it is above or below grade, but upon how it is designed.

To be accurate about the characteristics of your climate, you must do some investigating. It is worth the time: knowledge of your building's climate is just as important as knowledge of its site in determining the appropriate design. Fill in the proper information in the accompanying exercise, and you will have the particular items of information you or your designer will need.

Recording Your Own Climate Factors

Sources for climate data: local reporting station of the National Weather Service, or "Local Climatological Data, Annual Summary" for appropriate year and location, Publications, National Climate Center, Federal Building, Asheville, NC 28801.

● Heating and cooling degree days per year _____
_____

● Direction of prevailing seasonal winds _____
_____

● Seasonal humidity changes _____
_____

● Sun: Number of clear/cloudy days a year. (Sources: books on passive solar design or your state energy office.) _____
_____

● Sun: Rising/setting points and altitude figured at 9:00 AM, noon, and 4:00 PM during the summer and winter solstice and spring/fall equinox. (Same sources as above.) _____

Location

Realtors and lenders often remind clients that the three most important value criteria for any property are location, location, and location. Choosing the right area within a region for an earth sheltered house is certainly a matter of personal taste and convenience. If your goal is to save energy, you will doubtless emphasize the distance to workplaces and/or schools as a factor in choosing a location. Transportation energy, both daily and during construction, is just as important to save as heating energy.

In addition to standard criteria for choosing a location (schools, services, amenities), several factors take on more importance when an earth sheltered project is contemplated. The availability of resources and the potential impact of building codes and zoning ordinances should be investigated as you contemplate a location.

Availability of Resources
Determine which backup home heating fuels are available. Their relative cost and escalation rates might influence your selection of a location.

Your choice of structural materials, especially in rural areas, will be influenced by what is available nearby at a reasonable cost. For example, precast concrete plank must sometimes be shipped from so far away that the cost in dollars and in transportation energy is prohibitive.

The availability of public services can affect the value of anything you build, as well as the ultimate cost. If various utilities or services must be privately installed, your budget will have to reflect their cost from the beginning.

Investigate whether power and telephone lines are present. If natural gas is used in the area, are the lines in? Where will water come from and at what pressure? Is there police and fire protection? Is there a public sewer and water system? How deep are the sewer lines? If they are shallow, you might have to pump refuse up to their level.

Building Codes
Before you decide that the best location for an earth sheltered house is one in which no codes exist, allow us to put in a good word for building codes. They represent *minimum* standards, developed

Determining Resource Availability

Find out what specific resources are available in the general location you have identified. Use the worksheet to record what you discover.

Resource	Type	Availability	Estimated Cost and Escalation Rates
Backup fuels (Source: state energy office)	• oil • natural gas • propane • electricity • wood		
Materials (Source: local suppliers)	• concrete block • concrete plank • heavy timber • treated wood		
Utilities/Services (Source: local planning department)	• electric lines • gas lines • water • sewer • police • fire • hospital		

through sometimes tragic experience, to protect not only your health, welfare, and safety, but also that of subsequent owners. Consider codes to be an aid to good, safe design, not an obstacle. If code provisions are known and understood before you begin the design process, they can be met without too much difficulty.

Unlike zoning ordinances, building codes are similar around the country. Several nationally recognized model codes have been developed which, when adopted by states or localities, have the force of law. Another national set of standards, developed and administered by the U.S. Department of Housing and Urban Development (HUD), are called "Minimum Property Standards" (MPS). Any house built or financed under a HUD program, such as the Federal Housing Administration (FHA) insured loan program, must meet the MPS.

Codes are truly enforceable; no building permit is issued until the plans have been reviewed and approved for code compliance. Further, the inspector will check the building during construction and will grant an occupancy permit only when satisfied that the house is correctly built.

At this early stage, your main concern is whether or not a code is in effect for your locale and if so, which one it is. A design professional can be charged with the responsibility of meeting specific provisions, but having a working knowledge of the potential problem areas will be useful to you, especially if you intend to purchase stock plans that may have to be adapted.

Building code provisions were obviously not developed with earth sheltering in mind. Since their purpose is to protect the health and safety of building occupants, however, any variation should have a good reason. A very brief discussion of the code issues you may have to confront follows.

Fire Safety/Egress: For safety in case of fire, all codes require that adequate secondary means of exiting be provided for every habitable room (including bedrooms). Although "adequate" may be defined in various ways, in general an openable and accessible window to the outside, in addition to the door, is acceptable as a secondary means of egress.

Daylighting and Ventilation: With a tight structure and earth covering much of the wall area, designing for daylighting and ventilation becomes very important. Here again, code provisions designed for

conventional structures are appropriate for earth sheltered dwellings. Most codes contain a prescriptive requirement that habitable rooms have an aggregate window area equal to at least ten square feet or 10 percent of their floor area. Half of that window area must be openable for ventilation. Alternatively, you may substitute mechanical ventilation that provides two air changes per hour (bathrooms are considered differently).

An alternative to windows for ventilation purposes is thus allowed. Alternatives for the daylight windows provide are not so clear, however. Clerestories, skylights, and borrowed light from other rooms or interior courtyards are design possibilities, as long as the fire safety provisions previously mentioned have already been fulfilled.

Structural Soundness: The walls and footings in a fully earth sheltered house must often support roof loads in excess of five times the weight of a conventional roof. Fully bermed walls, especially two-story ones, must resist enormous sideways pressures. The model codes, since they cover commercial construction as well as residential, do offer some guidance; the MPS contain little.

Do not rely on the code official to evaluate the strength of your structure. *If you pay a professional to do nothing else, at least pay for engineering services on your structural system.* Here the code must be followed, and its standards for loading can best be met with proper engineering.

3—8. The open design and the clerestory windows at upper right help create an attractive light-filled interior in this two-story, 3,350—square foot Missouri house.

(Photo courtesy of *Earth Shelter Living*)

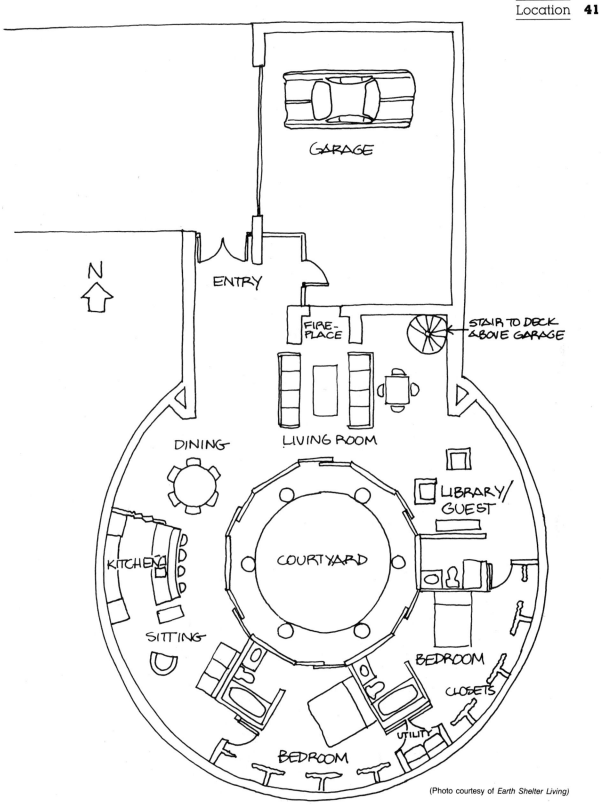

N

GARAGE

ENTRY

FIRE-
PLACE

STAIR TO DECK
ABOVE GARAGE

DINING

LIVING ROOM

COURTYARD

LIBRARY/
GUEST

KITCHEN

SITTING

BEDROOM

CLOSETS

UTILITY

BEDROOM

(Photo courtesy of *Earth Shelter Living*)

3–9. This simple floor plan shows a design that may not satisfy the fire exit provisions of a building code. Bedrooms have several exits, but none directly to the outside. With use of smoke alarms or other warning systems, this lovely design might be allowed a variance.

Waterproofing: If you waterproof your earth sheltered house to meet current model code standards, it will probably leak.

Building codes have not caught up with the phenomenon of earth-covered roofs and subsurface habitable space. Codes indicate various types of acceptable waterproof roofing materials in aboveground situations, but many of these materials may not perform satisfactorily when buried.

Waterproofing (or, more accurately, dampproofing) of below-grade walls is also covered in some of the model codes, but with little uniformity. Whereas in most circumstances the building codes provide not only minimum standards but also a kind of guide to good practice, such is not the case for waterproofing. On this point do not be satisfied with a system that only meets code.

Guardrails: If an earth-covered rooftop or tops of retaining walls are accessible to people, prudence would suggest railings or other barriers to prevent falls over an edge that could be ten feet or more above the ground. Though the codes' provisions regarding protection at a grade change vary in clarity and applicability, their intent is to prevent the inadvertent accident. Use of a guardrail or some acceptable alternative is a relatively minor design issue; the presence of such a provision should not pose a significant code problem.

Appeals: All of the national codes contain a kind of safety valve provision to deal with innovative situations. Called "Alternate Materials and Methods," these sections allow a building official to use some discretion. If you and the official cannot resolve a serious disagreement, however, an appeals process is also available, usually through the state. It is useful where unconventional or innovative buildings are in question, but it takes time.

Zoning Ordinances

Unlike building codes, zoning ordinances are always adopted and enforced locally by the governing body of the county or municipality, sometimes acting through a planning commission. The purpose of zoning is to regulate land use. Though more complicated in urban areas, zoning ordinances should be investigated in rural areas as well; lack of a building code does not necessarily imply a corresponding lack of zoning ordinances. Uses of lakeshore or riverfront may be regulated by zoning, as may the use of agricultural land.

There are no model national zoning systems, so the ordinances of individual localities vary considerably. Since their purposes are generally similar, however, there are some common considerations to explore that could inhibit your choice of a design or site.

Researching Building Codes

Find out if you are in a building code area and if so, which model code applies (source: your state building code office). If a code does apply, it would not hurt, even at this early stage, to contact the building official (through the county, municipality, or township) and ask for help in identifying sections of the code that require design attention. If you get him on your side by seeking his expert advice *before* you have a design, you might avoid future hassle.

● Model building code in my location: _____

_____

● Building official I'll be working with (name and phone): _____

_____

● Issues for design (secondary egress, ventilation, etc.): _____

_____

_____

3–10. In addition to the potential minimum height zoning violation, this earth sheltered house might be appraised at a lower value because of its incompatibility in size and shape with its neighbors.

Prohibition of "Basement Houses": Some zoning ordinances, devised to prevent unsightly as well as substandard housing, prohibit living in basement or cellar space. These regulations are often old ones, designed to eliminate the postwar phenomenon of building basements first, roofing them over, and then living permanently in an uncompleted house. Zoning officers usually consider such ordinances to be inappropriate for earth sheltered homes, but their existence can pose at least a temporary constraint.

Minimum Height Requirements: Again, these are likely to be old ordinances designed to promote uniformity of structures. A design with a low profile may require a variance. Not being able to secure one would suggest either a design modification to include some aboveground space, or another location.

Minimum Floor Area: A requirement that residences have a minimum amount of habitable space can be a problem if below-ground rooms are defined as basement space and thus excluded from floor area calculations. Check this possibility; it could be a serious problem. You may be able to convince the zoning officer to define your below-grade space as habitable if you point out that all code requirements for habitable space are being met. If not, find another location or an above-grade design.

Maximum Lot Coverage: Ordinances prescribing a maximum percentage of lot coverage by the building are designed to preserve some open space and limit the amount of runoff from hard surfaces. A single-story earth sheltered house may exceed the maximum, thus requiring a variance. Earth on a flat and accessible rooftop may meet the spirit, if not the letter, of the ordinance: a point of negotiation with the zoning officer.

Setbacks: Setback requirements regulate the open space allowed between a lot line and the structure itself; that is, the distance the house must be "set

3–11. The buried parts of the earth sheltered house at left exceed the hypothetical front and side setback allowances indicated; the aboveground portions do not. Whether this design would be acceptable would depend on the zoning officer.

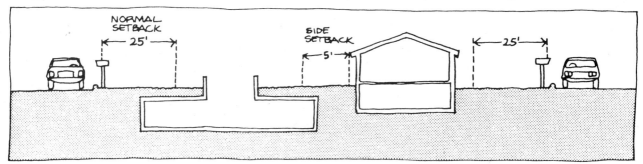

Researching Zoning Ordinances

Before deciding finally on a location, find the pertinent zoning officer (again through the county or municipality) and inquire whether any of the above regulations are in effect. Describe your intended project in case there are other unforeseen zoning obstacles. If you already own a site, record the data and note the possible constraints you discover.

● Prohibition of "Basement Houses" _____

_____

● Minimum height requirements _____

_____

● Minimum floor area _____

_____

● Maximum lot coverage _____

_____

● Setbacks _____

_____

● Solar Access _____

_____

back'' from the edges of the property. The valid purposes of these requirements include neighborhood uniformity, access between and around buildings, and protection for neighboring structures during excavation. The buried parts of your house could arguably violate the setback allowance and still preserve visual conformity and access between adjacent buildings even though the letter of the ordinance was not specifically observed. The zoning officer might allow a variance in such a case. If the excavation might actually endanger foundations of nearby buildings, you should look for another site.

Solar Access: A recent addition to the zoning ordinances of many municipalities, solar access ordinances are a potentially important benefit rather than an obstacle. If your project will be incorporating passive or active solar design, a solar access ordinance offers a process that can protect you from the eventuality that future buildings nearby would obstruct your access to sunshine.

If you are already locked into a specific site, the foregoing regional and locational factors will indicate whether it is impossible, uneconomical but possible, or well suited for earth sheltering. Before deciding finally, consider the site-specific information in the next chapter.

Chapter 4

Site Selection

The focus of your site considerations can now be trained on a narrower field. Having investigated regional climate and locational resources and regulations, you are ready to look at the specific factors that determine earth sheltering's suitability on a given site.

The exercises suggested in this chapter lead to two goals: finding the right site, and completing the first part of your program, a comprehensive site description. Do not be confused by the order in which the exercises are presented. Some are designed to lead you through a mapping process that need only be done for your chosen site; if you already own your site, you will be able to complete the exercises in the order they appear. If you are still looking, however, read through the site mapping exercises as they come along; they pinpoint items you should be checking out on your candidate sites. It would be needless work to map every site you consider. Once you acquire your site, mapping it according to the exercises will be a good discipline for getting to know it very well.

Site Evaluation

Microclimate

The regions drawn in broad strokes on the climate map in figure 3–7 are based on quite generalized climate data. Your particular microclimate, that is, the climate your home will experience on your site, may well differ from that of the region as a whole. Your site's specific potential for energy savings through earth sheltering may correspondingly vary from the generalized potential of the region.

To identify the problems and opportunities presented by a site's microclimate, look for topographical features that may affect the site's sun, wind, and humidity patterns. For example, a south-facing slope will be warmer than a north-facing one, because sun falls on it for more hours each day and because it is protected from colder north winds. Trees or adjacent buildings can also modify temperatures on a site, both by shading and by channeling winds.

Low spots will be cooler and more moist than

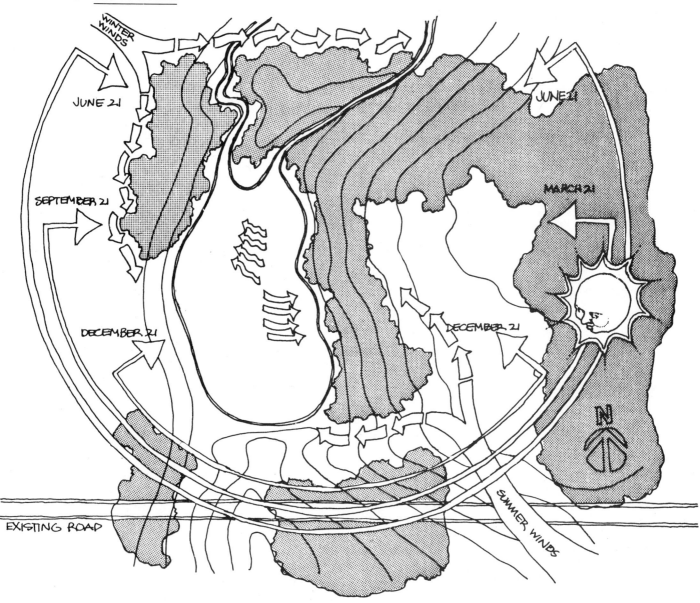

4-1. Specific features on this hypothetical site affect the microclimate. The pond cools by evaporation, and onshore breezes during the day will cool as well. Trees (shaded areas) buffer prevailing northwest winter winds and channel summer winds. Contour lines indicate larger slopes on the east and south sides of the pond. For view and solar access combined, however, the north side of the pond would be the best building site.

high spots. A site located on a shore will experience cool breezes heading offshore at night and toward the land during the day. On a steep slope, wind is likely to go upslope in the daytime and downslope at night.

Figure 4-1 is a map of a hypothetical site. The contour lines show slopes on all sides of the small pond. Vegetation (shaded areas) occurs on the north and east sides of the pond. The microclimate on the north side of the pond, a good potential building

site, would be warmer in the winter than the generalized climate data would indicate, because the trees and southerly slope would shelter a building from cold winds and an exposed south-facing wall would receive winter sunlight all day.

The summer microclimate would correspondingly be cooler than normal for the area, because summer breezes, though partially shielded from the southeast, would probably still be channeled around the trees and cross the cool waters of the pond before striking the building. Summer sun would warm the building, of course, but shading provided by the existing vegetation on the east and west sides would help significantly in keeping the building cool.

Surface Conditions

Topography: To evaluate the suitability of the site's surface contours for an earth sheltered house, you need only consider the two extremes of topography, flat and sloping. Varied topography may affect the breeze patterns, but it is not otherwise a problem; it is not likely that a house would be large enough to cover more than one slope.

A flat site does not necessarily rule out earth sheltered design. Although costly, it is possible to construct a one-level building at or slightly below grade level and then build up earth around it. The building could also be fully recessed or covered.

A sloping site offers more opportunity than a flat one. It is natural to want to concentrate the building's openings in the same direction as that of the slope, so that the shape of the building interrupts the shape of the land as little as possible.

The orientation of the slope then becomes an important factor in site selection and subsequent design choice. A south-facing slope is the ideal topography, in most climates, for a passive solar earth sheltered design. In the summer, as figure 4-3 indicates, the amount of sunlight striking the combined east and west elevations is equal to that striking the south face. In other words, only half of the summer day's sunlight strikes the south side. Protecting the east and west sides is thus a good cooling strategy.

In winter, sunlight conveniently strikes the south side for a much greater proportion of the day, so south glass (with an overhang to shade it from the summer's high midday sun) is optimum in both seasons for a climate with hot summers and cold winters. Exposing the south wall correspondingly means protecting the north wall. Figure 4-2 shows how the winter climate interacts with a south-facing design.

Although other slope orientations should not be eliminated from consideration, designs for these other exposures confront a more complex set of trade-offs. Figure 4-3 illustrates the effects of sun angles at varying seasons on east and west exposures. A single exposed wall facing east is probably the next best alternative to south for taking advantage of passive solar gain. The western exposure is a close second, because the time of day that heat is

entering the structure is the time when everyone is home to enjoy it. In warm seasons or climates, however, western exposure becomes a problem. Controlling sunlight entry by means of overhangs is more difficult because the angle of late afternoon sun is low and because the late afternoon sun's heat enters at what is already the hottest time of day.

Last, and least suitable in colder climates, is the northerly orientation. In warm climates the better

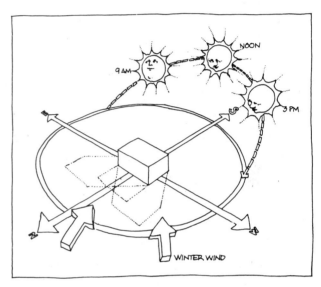

4–2. The relationship of sun and wind to a south-facing house in the winter. Opening the house to the south in winter captures most of a winter day's sun; north and west sides can be protected with earth against cold northwest winds.

4–3. Imagine this house facing first east, then west. Note that much sunlight falls on east and west sides in the summer; in winter, very little.

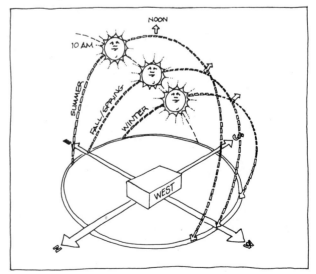

AERIAL PERSPECTIVE FROM THE NORTH EAST

4—4. "House for a North Slope," designed by architect Malcolm Wells of Brewster, MA, is drawn looking south up the slope. This perspective shows the roof slant that both protects against cold winds and provides the opportunity for high south-facing windows.

(Drawing courtesy of Malcolm Wells)

slope orientation is the north-facing one, though the glass would not necessarily be placed on the north side.

There are exceptions to all such statements, and in the case of earth sheltering, most of those exceptions are made feasible by good design. A lovely example of a north-facing slope solution for a northern climate is in *Underground Plans Book—1* by architect Malcolm Wells, one of the earliest and most thoughtful spokesmen for earth sheltering. About his north-facing house design, and the whole north/south issue in general, Wells says: "South-facing houses do get both view and sunlight through the same window but they also get squinting, glare, highly visible smudges on the glass, and faded fabrics. This north-facing house avoids much of that by bringing its south light (and solar energy) in high—glarelessly—and opening to a view in the more pleasant northward direction."

The steepness of the slope is another factor to consider. If your grade rises more than three feet for every linear foot of surface, your project will probably be too expensive. Retaining walls will have to be very high, and heavy construction equipment might not be able to approach the building site.

Nevertheless, earth sheltering is probably a better solution than any other for a steep slope. Earth sheltered building systems like that of architectural/engineering firm Architerra, Inc. of Washington, DC, for example, actually stabilize the slopes on which the homes are built. Architerra is constructing multifamily units on slopes as steep as 40 percent.

Surface Drainage: In general the direction and flow of rainwater (especially spring runoff) will not affect actual site selection, but it will affect where the building is placed on the site.

You should naturally avoid building in the path

HOUSE FOR A NORTH SLOPE

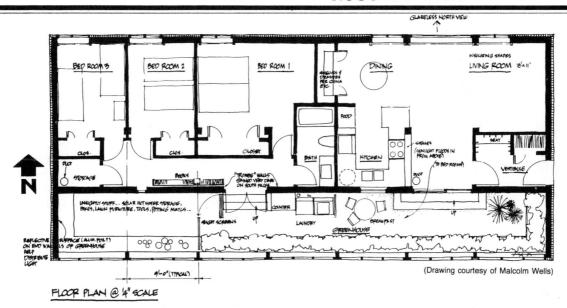

(Drawing courtesy of Malcolm Wells)

4—5. The floor plan for Malcolm Wells's elevational design illustrates his separation of solar access (into the greenhouse on the south and through vertical glass above) from visual access to the north view.

HOUSE FOR A NORTH SLOPE

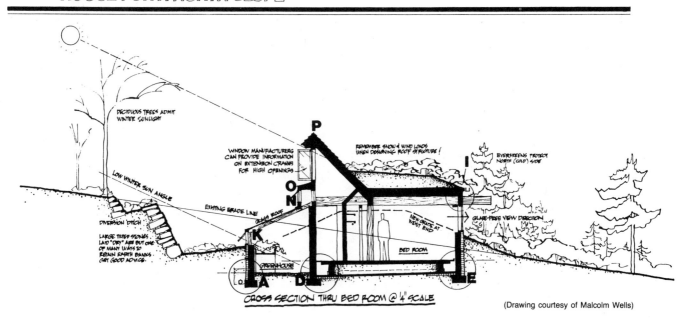

(Drawing courtesy of Malcolm Wells)

4—6. Cross-section through the bedroom of the Wells house.

of seasonal or regular flows. All surface drainage should flow *away* from the house, preferably not onto a neighbor's lot.

Neighborhood Compatibility: If your anticipated site is in a residential area, the neighborhood itself is one more surface condition for consideration. It is impossible and undesirable to quote a few pat rules on the most compatible relationship between a new structure and its neighbors—impossible because all rules have their exceptions; undesirable because architectural advancements are often made by breaking the established rules.

The new must consider the old, but the successful relationship could conceivably be one of contrast as often as it is one of harmony. Only a good designer can do both well. It is possible to say that if the aesthetic result of your earth sheltering efforts looks like a pile of sod and railroad ties from the street, it probably will neither contrast successfully nor harmonize with, for example, a turn-of-the-century Greek revival neighborhood. Your personal relationships with your new neighbors may not be very harmonious either.

On the pragmatic side, consider the effect of compatibility on the value of your house, appraised both when you apply for financing and when you eventually sell to someone else. If your structure differs significantly in size, shape, cost, design, or exterior finish from its surroundings, its appraised

4—7. Greenhouse interior of "House for a North Slope," looking west towards bermed west wall.

(Drawing courtesy of Malcolm Wells)

Architerra Project at Vail

Architerra, Inc.
Dennis Blair, architect/Charles G. Woods, solar designer

(Drawing courtesy of Architerra, Inc.)

4—8. Drawing of a duplex in Vail, CO, soon to be built. The design and reinforced earth system for slope stabilization are by Architerra, Inc.

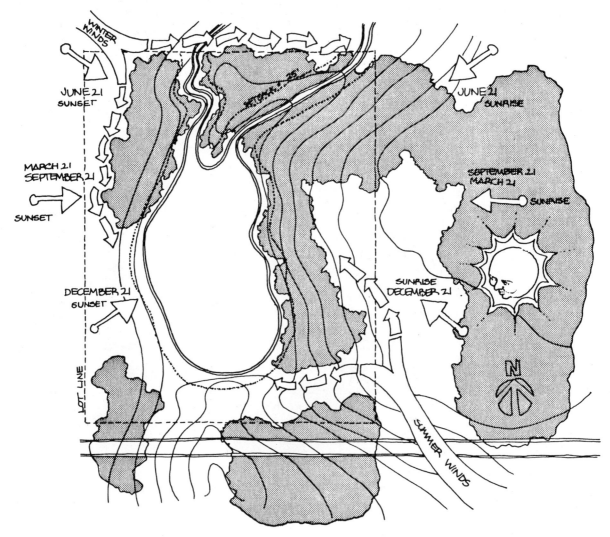

4—9. Sample site map, showing only surface features. Contour lines showing topography are most accurately drawn by professional surveyors. Indicating high and low points and slope directions would be a sufficient alternative to contour lines for an owner's site map.

value could be reduced. Financing officers frown at loan applicants whose homes would be difficult to resell if the owner defaults on the loan. A "sore thumb" on a residential street would cause you problems if you need to obtain financing.

When selecting a site, then, take the context of the neighborhood into account. The public side of your house should be "well mannered"; if it is completely out of step with an established neighborhood, you make either the other houses or your own look foolish.

To sum up, there are really no surface conditions that would totally eliminate earth sheltering as a design option. Nevertheless, conditions like steep slopes or poorly located drainage paths may make it uneconomical.

An important surface feature not mentioned above, according to Malcolm Wells, is "the community of living creatures already there, the most important of which may well be the topsoil itself. All the other creatures depend upon it for sustenance. How that topsoil is moved, stockpiled, and respread is critical to the success of the job. Other important creatures include trees, shrubs, grasses, and wildlife, and a proper site survey will show all major trees and plant areas along with the contour lines and the boundaries."

Site Mapping, Surface Features

If you own a site, you now have enough information to begin preparing the site description. (A site *plan* will appear later, and show where you or your designer intend to place the house.)

The site description, like a site plan, is essentially an overgrown map, except that unlike the site plan, it will not show the proposed house. Begin the site map by locating surface features.

Pace out and measure the boundaries of the site; draw your map to scale. Using graph paper will make your task easier.

The features to include at this point are:

- boundaries, lengths, and widths of the lot
- high points, low points, slopes
- existing vegetation (trees, shrubs)
- direction of seasonal prevailing breezes
- sunrise and sunset points at summer solstice, winter solstice, and spring/fall equinox
- access points, utilities
- any easements, covenants, or setbacks discovered in your conversations with the current owner or the zoning officer.

Draw the map to encompass not only the actual lot, but also neighbors' homes, the street, and any nearby features (like a pond or an unsightly view) that might influence your eventual design. Label and describe each feature.

It is usually not necessary for you as the owner to produce a site map that is accurate down to the last detail. The exercise is suggested here as a device to help you acquire an intimate knowledge of the problems and opportunities of a given site and to communicate information to a designer. If an accurate and comprehensive map is what you need, then seek the professional help of a surveyor.

The surveyor will describe and document surface conditions. His survey would also reveal whatever is recorded, both about the surface and the subsurface, in any documents already on file. Surveyors are registered and can be located through the Yellow Pages. An architect can also recommend and direct a surveyor. The charge will range anywhere from $500 to $1,500, so have one done only on your chosen site.

As an alternative, look for existing surveys or plat maps of candidate sites by calling the planning department or recorder of deeds of your city or county. Existing surveys will show the location, ownership, and surface conditions of your site and

will include the contour lines that describe the topography.

Subsurface Conditions

Soils: The conclusion about climates also holds true for soils: earth sheltered houses could conceivably be built in any soil conditions, but some soils are definitely more suitable than others.

The most suitable kind of soil to build in has two primary characteristics: it compacts well for good bearing capacity, and it is permeable, that is, it will drain quickly.

Good bearing capacity is obviously important because of the weight of the structure being placed on it. Not so immediately obvious is the extra cost for footings that a poorly compacting soil invites. The soil's firmness provides a counterpressure to the weight of the building. When this counterpressure is inadequate, the footings that support the building must be larger. A designer will make the footings large (and expensive) if the soil's bearing capacity is not good, and a prudent designer will draw footings extra large (and extra expensive) if the capacity is not specifically known.

The soil's permeability, or capacity to drain, is an important factor both in structural design and in the success of a waterproofing system. Water that does not drain away quickly builds up pressure against walls and increases the weight of the roof. In addition, these pressures look for outlets—through the waterproofing and into the building.

The worst soils to build in, as a general rule, are cohesive soils, like clays or organic soils. Organic soils are permeable but compact poorly; clay compacts well but is not permeable. In fact, some clays expand when wet, exerting enormous sideways pressure against the walls of a subsurface building.

4–10. The cost of concrete, steel reinforcing, and labor for the footings (shaded areas) in House A on the left would be approximately $1,400 in 1982. For House B, designed for a poorly compacting soil, the cost would be approximately $4,400—nearly four times as great.

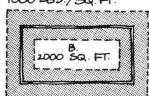

category	type	qualifiers	suitability
cohesionless	gravels sands	very loose loose	good drainage but may need compaction for adequate bearing.
		med. dense dense very dense	excellent—good drainage, good bearing, low lateral pressures
	silty sands clayey sands		will depend on whether cohesive or cohesionless elements dominate its behavior. should generally be workable unless soft or loose conditions prevail.
cohesive	silts clays	very soft soft	careful evaluation needed.
		med. stiff stiff very stiff hard	should present no particular problems structurally. drainage of high water requires granular backfill. septic tank system can have problems.
		expansive	avoid
	highly organic soils	peat humus swamp soils	would probably require extensive replacement of soil or use of special foundation techniques.

(From *Earth Sheltered Housing Design: Guidelines, Examples and References*, by the Underground Space Center at the University of Minnesota. Copyright 1979 by the University of Minnesota. Reprinted by permission of Van Nostrand Reinhold Company)

4—11. Suitability of various soils for earth sheltered construction. For the sake of clarity, the soil categories in the chart express more uniformity than would be found in real soils, which are often mixtures. Only a soils investigation will reveal the truth about your subsurface.

A house built in a clay that periodically expands with moisture will be expensive. Structural strength must be increased to resist the lateral pressures, and a zone of permeable soil around the building may be needed, both to drain off water near the envelope quickly and to allow for a lighter structure. It is possible to build in clay if the climate is such that the clay never gets wet.

The soils to avoid, then, are those that trap water, that expand when wet, or that have poor bearing capacity. The best soils to build in are granular soils like sand and gravel; both compact well, and both are permeable.

Certain soft rock, like sandstone, can be excavated relatively inexpensively. Very large boulders or layers of hard rock near the surface would require blasting, a costly process.

Besides bearing capacity and permeability, other soil properties should be investigated, but these will be more likely to affect your design than your actual choice of site. Such properties as frost sensitivity, shrink/swell potential, settlement characteristics, acidity, and moisture content will be specifically tested later during a soils engineer's investigation.

Water Table: Putting part of any house below the depth at which the ground is saturated would be hard to justify. It can be and is done fairly frequently with large commercial buildings but is not economical for a single residential project. So stay out of a swamp, and look for sites where the water table is at least several feet below your anticipated footing depth. Well drillers in the area will have general information on the water table; it will be discovered specifically during a soils test.

To sum up, subsurface conditions that would

eliminate or discourage earth sheltering as an option are soils with poor compaction or permeability or near-surface rock strata or water tables.

Soils Test

The specific subsurface information necessary for a complete site description can be discovered only by conducting a soils investigation. The professional needed is a soils engineer, who will either dig some trenches or bore deep holes to obtain soil samples illustrating subsurface conditions. Your architect can arrange and direct the soils engineer's work; if you are arranging it yourself, find a registered professional engineer who specializes in soils by looking under "Engineers-Soils" in the Yellow Pages.

To arrange the test, call the engineer and describe the site briefly, indicating your intentions as to the design and possible location of the house on the site. Discuss the number, locations, and depth of the borings or trenches. In general, two test bores are a minimum, one where the building might be located, and the other where a well or septic system would be placed. A boring depth of 10 feet below footing depth, or approximately 20 feet, is recommended. The charge will be about $500 for two borings.

Soil samples will be obtained and water levels investigated at the site. The owner will receive the resulting report, and copies will go to the architect and/or structural engineer. The purpose of the soil report is to describe subsurface conditions and to recommend how to deal with the soil findings. The report should include:

- depth of topsoil
- location of groundwater level
- bearing capacity of soil
- alternative types and/or depth of foundation
- data on soil properties for evaluating earth pressures and construction methods
- predictions of soil settlement
- potential problems concerning adjacent properties
- percolation (drainage rate) test results

Site Mapping, Subsurface Features

Enter the location of the test bores on the site map you have begun. The information associated with the bores will help you place the house. For example, on our hypothetical site map, figure 4-9, the soils test may have revealed that the north side of the pond is an area of highly organic soils, with a water table near the surface. Though solar angles and view make this an ideal building site, the soils information could prevent a costly mistake in siting.

Your site map is now done. Further site description to complete the analysis process will be suggested at the end of this chapter.

resources to which you simply do not have access. For example, available lots are included and described in the Multiple Listing Service (MLS) just as houses are. In addition to such vital characteristics as water and sewer availability, size, zoning classification, and cost, the MLS may include supplemental information that will help sell the property, such as southern exposure.

Realtors tend to specialize in particular geographic areas, so their personal network of information is an even greater resource. They may know of lots available for purchase that are not currently listed; their colleagues may know of others. Such personal inventories and the MLS are far superior to your own possibilities, which are limited to newspaper advertisements and door-to-door adventuring.

Finding the right realtor may take some time. Few realtors actually specialize in energy-efficient construction, unless they happen to be working with an energy-efficient builder. Probably the best search method is simply to ask some of the larger realty firms in your chosen area to recommend a knowledgeable person. Alternatively, discuss what you need with a realtor you already know and trust.

You will receive the best service when you work with only one realtor, and he will show you his best sites first. Since lots move on and off the market more slowly than houses do, waiting for a better site may not be as good an alternative as looking in another area.

The price of a lot relative to a house is small, so the realtor's commission will also be small. He will give you better attention if he knows you mean business. If you are a casual looker, inform him. He will watch for the right property, but his attention may be sporadic.

Site Acquisition

Locating Potential Sites

Having identified and researched the resources and regulations regarding suitable locations, your next step is to define some search areas. Then begin looking for a realtor.

Working with a real estate professional will save time and a good deal of footwork. A realtor has

A combination realtor/builder may give you the best service of all because of the larger amount of business your patronage could bring. A builder who works with a realtor may already have some available building sites identified.

The realtor is paid on a commission basis. The seller usually pays 10 percent of the purchase price to his own realtor to have the lot sold; half of this fee will go to the buyer's realtor.

Assessing Particular Sites

There is nothing magic about finding the right site. The worksheet further on in this chapter will be useful for comparing candidate sites: the factors listed should all be taken into consideration as you assess a site. Showing the list to your realtor before you select sites to visit will help you describe the site conditions you are seeking.

Begin your evaluation of candidate sites with the *surface* conditions. At each site you visit, use as your criteria the climate and location factors discussed in chapter 3. You know the general climate information already, and the realtor can give you general information about local resources, codes, and zoning; that is part of his or her job.

Site-specific surface factors such as microclimate, topography, drainage, and neighborhood can be easily observed. If you look in the fall or winter, you will see surface contours that might be obscured by summer foliage. Visits in spring or during a rainfall will show potential surface drainage problems. You will probably eliminate several sites this way.

When you proceed to investigating the *subsurface*, do not immediately call the soils engineer. Local builders will know a good deal about soils and water table. Indeed, if a builder has platted (charted) the land you are considering, he may already have done a soils test to qualify the sites for FHA financing.

You could also check with your county recorder of deeds or planning body for plat maps or surveys showing possible subsurface obstructions and, if you are lucky, the results of previous soils tests. The local office of the Soil Conservation Service of the Department of Agriculture could be another avenue for generalized subsurface information. The subsurface data you are gathering will not make a soils test unnecessary, but it might save having to pay for several.

Take your architect to see your final choices. Between you, determine which is the best from what you see and know. You are now ready to make an offer and even to sign a purchase agreement for your first choice. The report of the soils engineer could change your mind about the site, however, so make sure your purchase agreement clearly states that your purchase is contingent on acceptable findings of a soils test. Then go ahead and make arrangements (through your architect if you wish) for the soils test, as described earlier.

Financing Site Acquisition

There are several ways to buy a lot. First, you can pay cash. A cash sales contract will be signed by you and the seller, and the title to the property will be transferred to you. Having a new deed drawn up and registered calls for the services of a lawyer. Once you own the site, you can use its value as the equivalent of the down payment on your home mortgage.

A lot can also be purchased by means of a contract for deed. The contract, executed between you and the seller, is an instrument that specifies the terms (interest rate, duration, payment amount) under which you agree to pay for the lot over time. This method is often called private financing; the seller is in effect underwriting your purchase. In contrast to a mortgage, you do not receive fee title (the deed) to the property until the contract terms have been met. Thus, if you plan to build right away, a contract for deed is not a good alternative. The deed will not change hands until the contract is paid off, and you cannot build on a lot you do not actually own.

The third option is to consider the lot as part of the new house price and, working through a builder, use interim financing to pay for both the lot and house together. This is the most common way to finance site acquisition. You sign a purchase agreement for the house and lot and secure your permanent financing. On the strength of this, the builder arranges an interim or construction loan and uses it to buy the lot himself and build the house. Then he sells lot and house back to you in a package and pays off his loan with the proceeds. (More discussion on financing appears in chapter 8.)

Mortgages are rarely written for lots alone. If they are, the required down payment could be as high as 70 percent.

Site Description

Once you have identified and acquired your site, refer to the worksheets earlier in this chapter to

Assessing Potential Sites

	PON D SITE (example)		
Accessibility	(access from existing road not built; construction equipment no problem)		
Resources/Services (See worksheet, chapter 3)	(water/sewer: NO fire: yes electric: available oil, gas: NO concrete products: nearby)		
Building codes (See worksheet, chapter 3)	(no code in effect)		
Zoning ordinances (See worksheet, chapter 3)	(25-ft. setback)		
Microclimate (See worksheet, chapter 4)	(pond cools; slope + trees deflect NW winds)		
Topography (See worksheet, chapter 4)	(slopes in all directions toward pond)		
Drainage	(toward pond: probably poor at north end)		
Neighborhood	(no houses in view)		
Soil	(local builder say ok; no test yet)		
Water table	(possibly near surface at north end — generally 50-100 ft., say well drillers)		
Other comments	(lovely pond, woods, PRIVACY!!!).		

Completing Site Description

The remaining information needed to complete a comprehensive site description cannot necessarily be drawn on a map. Referring to your notes concerning climate, resources, and regulations (chapter 3 worksheets), or those made while assessing po-tential sites, list on the worksheet those factors that will be important for you and your designer to keep in mind. This list plus your site map comprise your total site description.

Important Features	Description

Climate/Microclimate
    heating, cooling degree days
    humidity
    sun	

Resources/Services
    fuels
    materials
    utilities	

Building code provisions	
Zoning requirements	

prepare your site map. If you have owned your site all along and have been double checking its characteristics through the increasingly specific levels of evaluation, you will already have completed the map portion of your site description.

You now have a better site profile in your mind than most owners ever have, and that is all to the good. Your site, your way of life, and your design are inseparable elements, each influencing the kind of house you want. Keep your site image in your head as you proceed to consider your living needs and your actual design in the next chapters.

Chapter 5

Design Preparation

By the end of this chapter, you will have completed the entire program for your house. The first half, your site description, involved external factors that would apply to anyone owning your particular site. The other half of your program will be concerned with the internal, personal assessments that tailor the design to your needs.

Identifying Shelter Goals

If you are becoming impatient for a design, this additional stage in your home planning may appear tiresome. Actually, the goal-setting process is likely to be quite absorbing. It allows you to look in an organized manner at the way you live and, even better, at the way you want to live. The written analysis helps communicate your goals to someone else quickly, neatly, and honestly. After all, unless you know what you do *not* want, you might get precisely that.

Finally, the exercise will help you to identify and resolve areas where your design tastes, goals,

pocketbook, and site might contradict one another. Imagine getting inextricably into design before discovering, for example, that lurking within the professed earth sheltered enthusiast in your family is a two-story brick colonial heart.

Of course, the challenges posed by some contradictions can give birth to some stunning and creative solutions, so do not be afraid of them; just make sure they surface. Contradictions can cost enormous amounts of time and money if not identified at an early stage.

Personal Analysis

When you are working from a clean slate to analyze your needs and wants, it is easiest to start thinking in categories. Ask yourselves what you want the house to do for you, what it should look like, and what kinds of rooms you want. Forget about practicalities for a time and express your deepest feelings about shelter. (The exercises that follow are adapted from client worksheets used by Gerald Allen, St. Paul architect.)

Wish Lists and Problem Lists

Wish Lists: Have each member of the household write out his or her wants and needs: a kind of shopping list of wishes. To get started, ponder these attitude questions and then use the first column in the worksheet to record and compose the "wishes" growing out of your responses.

In imagining what you want the house to do, consider the following:

- What do you think are the most important functions of a house? Of the landscape around (and above) it?
- Do you like being knowledgeable about and involved in its operation?
- How do you feel about maintenance?
- What do you want outside space to do for you?
- What should the transition areas (entryways, porches, courtyards) between the outside and the inside be like?

As a way to focus on how your house should look, find at least six adjectives to describe your ideal home. Think of what you like: chrome, glass, and a spare, clean look, for example? Perhaps you prefer a warmer atmosphere, with plenty of wood and stone. What should your house do either to or for your site: blend in or stand out?

What kinds of rooms do you like: open and large, or small and cozy? What kinds of activities would you require spaces to accommodate? If you wanted to add space in the future, what would it be?

Problem Lists: Unlike the wish lists, your problem lists should be very practical. In the second column of the worksheet, list the kinds of things from your experiences that you want to avoid in your new home. Note everything, no matter how large or small: poor electrical outlet location, for example, or lack of privacy, too much maintenance or no good place for plants.

	Wishes	Problems
What the house should do (Performance)		
What the house should look like (Design)		
The kinds of rooms I want (Room List)		

Household Goals

Use the next worksheet to organize your goals into the same three categories used before. What you are doing is translating your somewhat diffuse feelings about the house into more specific terms regarding performance, design, and desired rooms.

These specific household goals should lead off the second, personal half of your program. An architect would certainly want to discuss and develop them further with you.

Goals	
Performance	
Design	
Rooms (size, arrangement)	

Resulting Household Goals

When you all gather to compare your individual lists, you should enjoy a lively and revealing session. Combine and distill your lists until you can write down collective goals for the house, noting any differences of opinion among you.

Room Arrangements

The spaces in a house fall into three general activity categories:
- working (kitchen, garage, entries)
- living (living, dining, family rooms)
- sleeping (bedrooms and adjacent baths)

Room Arrangements

Play with the arrangement of your listed spaces in relation to one another. To avoid getting bogged down with actual dimensions or shapes, use "bubbles"—sketchy circles that indicate activity areas—rather than straight-ruled edges that describe specific rooms. Use the worksheet to sketch arrangements until you have private/public spaces and circulation working together the way you want. Then reconsider your arrangement from the standpoint of light, egress, solar orientation, and the specifics of your site.

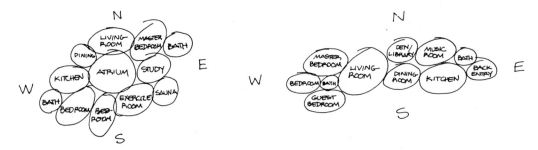

5—1. Sample bubble diagrams of room arrangements.

Room arrangements

Some activities are shared or public; others require privacy. Some logically occur in adjacent spaces; others should be in separated areas. For efficient use of the total enclosed area of the house, space used only for circulation should be kept to a minimum.

Earth sheltering itself places some constraints on room arrangements. Access to light and to the outside should be provided for habitable rooms, and plenty of storage space will be needed to make up for the lack of a basement. The siting of the house on your lot may suggest certain arrangements as well. If the spot you have tentatively chosen is steeply sloping, a two-story house may be in order. Certainly the position of your habitable rooms will be influenced by their orientation towards the sun.

Assessing Resources

Financial Capability

Though it is too early at this point to predict what the project will cost, the time is right for assessing what you can realistically afford to spend. The maximum amount you can commit to the project is the *total* project budget. This amount is not to be confused with the construction budget (the contractor's fee). The project budget will also include design fees, legal fees, furnishings, equipment, moving, and land costs. Make sure you distinguish between the two budgets in your planning—especially in your conversations with lenders and architects.

Assuming you will finance the house at least partially through a mortgage, your total project budget can be discovered by calculating what you can afford for the down payment and for monthly mortgage payments.

Use the following worksheets for making your personal informal estimates of what you can afford. List all of your assets under "Available Funds" *except* those you will not or cannot liquidate for a down payment. (A complete listing of assets will later be requested by the lender as part of a mortgage application.)

The result is the amount of down payment you can afford. (Most of the nonconstruction costs can be included in your financing, but many are paid before the mortgage or even a possible construction loan is approved. So even though you could be borrowing to cover these costs later, you may have spent this much cash before you can write a check for the down payment.)

Computing Available Down Payment

Available funds:
Total the following items:

- Equity in an already owned site $ _____

- Equity in present home   _____

- Savings, savings certificates   _____

- Investments (current value)   _____

- Insurance (cash surrender value)   _____

- Other available funds (like personal loan)   _____

     Total Funds $ _____

Cash Expenses: Subtract your project's expected cash expenses (nonconstruction costs):

- Financing: credit check, appraisal fee (chapter 8) $ _____

- Equipment, furniture, decorating   _____

- Moving expenses   _____

- Professional fees: soils tests and surveys (chapter 4), legal fees, design fees (chapter 5)   _____

- Building permit or utility hookup fees (chapter 7)   _____

- Allowance for contingencies   _____

- Other expected expenses   _____

     Total Cash Expense $ _____

     Down Payment $ _____

Computing Monthly Housing Budget

Monthly Mortage Payments: The general rule of thumb lenders have traditionally used for calculating your monthly payment ability is that your annual costs for principal, interest, taxes, and insurance (PITI) should not exceed 25 to 28 percent of your total annual income.

To find the PITI you can support, start with your total annual income:

- combined take-home pay $_____
- rents $_____
- dividends $_____
- interest $_____
- alimony $_____
- child support $_____
- other *stable* income $_____

           TOTAL $_____

Determine what 28 percent of the total is and divide the result by 12. The result is the monthly amount available *only* for PITI; it does not include coverage of such other monthly housing expenses as utilities or maintenance.

Total Monthly Housing Expense: Another approach is to figure the total monthly amount you can spend for all housing expense. This time add up your monthly income, including your combined household take-home pay and any other stable monthly income. Then subtract current average *non-housing* monthly expenses (car payments, food, educational expenses). The result will be the amount you can apply to regular mortage payments (PITI) and to other housing-related expenses.

Remember, the more your design saves energy costs and maintenance, the more money you can shift over into the PITI category. We will discuss this potential in greater detail in chapter 8.

Computing Total Project Budget

Having calculated both your down payment and your monthly mortage payment capability, you need only determine your borrowing limit before arriving at your maximum budget for the project.

Borrowing Limit: Using either the standard mortgage tables available in bookstores or from your friendly financial advisor, determine how much of a mortgage loan you can afford based on what you can spend monthly for PITI. (This would be a convenient occasion for paying a preliminary visit to a lender. While discussing your financial capability, sound him out regarding your tentative plans.)

Borrowing Limit $_____

To the amount you can borrow, add the amount you can supply in down payment.

Down Payment $_____

Total Project Budget $_____

The result is a good estimate of your total project budget. Consider it an absolute maximum figure and aim for total costs that are somewhat lower so that unforeseen contingencies will not bankrupt your project.

What is affordable to you is naturally of intense interest to your architect, so plan to include the total project budget amount in your program.

Available Time

Having any new house built requires an investment of another personal resource: your time. When the kind of house contemplated is relatively new to the building industry, your time investment may be much greater.

As you have already guessed, the planning process is longer. All facets of site, design, construction, and landscaping need to be thought out in advance, as they must be integrated even more intimately than for a conventional structure. Locating expertise may well take you longer. You may find yourself in extended conversations with people whose involvement would be brief for a conventional house: for example, the building codes official, the zoning officer, and the lender.

If your strategy includes doing most of the actual construction yourself, be prepared for a full-time undertaking. Arguing for the owner-builder approach is Robert Roy, an earth sheltered owner, builder, and author in West Chazy, New York. Mr. Roy points out in a paper given at an Underground Space Center conference in 1980:

> One-third of the "average" American's after-tax income is devoted to Shelter, usually rent or mortage payments. If a man works from the age of 20 to the age of 65, it could be legitimately argued that he has put in fifteen years just to keep a roof over his head. With six months' work (and $8,500 in materials), he and his family could have built their own house.
>
> "All that is fine and dandy for writers, golf pros, and other layabouts," people tell me. "But I'm a *working* man. I can't afford to take six months off to build my own house."
>
> I reply that to save fourteen and a half years of work, they can't afford *not* to build. . . .

Whether or not you are swayed by Roy's argument, compare your available time, enthusiasm, and persistence level with the demands that will be placed on them. Determine which parts of the process you will realistically find time to do.

Knowledge, Skills, and Experience
Building a good earth sheltered house requires high levels of expertise in design, construction techniques, and scheduling of the building process.

Designing safely but still economically for the loads on a structure requires accurate calculation of stresses. Waterproofing products, among other materials in an earth sheltered project, must be selected correctly and applied with skill. Solving problems on a job site and managing a complex work schedule are easier tasks when the manager is experienced in earth sheltered construction.

The above is not intended to invite discouragement, only realism. Evaluate your own time, skills, and experience—realistically—along with your other resources, and plan to include the pertinent information in your program.

Completing Your Program

Although the process of gathering and analyzing personal information has been long and complex, the statement should be straightforward and concise: not more than two or three pages. The points can be elaborated and developed verbally.

An outline of the topics in your program's personal half, derived from the worksheets you completed earlier in this chapter, is suggested below:

- performance goals
- design goals
- room list, including size (small, medium, large) and possible arrangement
- total project budget
- intended owner participation

Choosing Professional Assistance

In its early development, earth sheltering was adopted eagerly by proponents of self-reliance who preferred, like Thoreau, to take a direct, hands-on approach to the provision of their food and shelter. Rob Roy is a good example. Even if they had wished to hire professional help, few architects and even fewer contractors knew much more about subterranean design or construction than they did.

This is not the case any more. Professionals are now showing interest and gaining experience that is worth your investment, having been stimulated and encouraged by the work of pioneering designers like Malcolm Wells and Don Metz, early builders like Earth Shelter Corporation of America and Terra-Dome Corporation, and researchers like Kenneth Labs and the Underground Space Center's director, Raymond Sterling.

Although we will discuss other alternatives, we believe you need professional assistance in both design and construction. On the practical side, you are buying experience that can save time, of course, but also, in the long run, money. You will avoid design mistakes—and in an earth sheltered house these can be more costly than you might think. A well-designed, well-built house will hold its value; furthermore, a prospective second owner may not be interested in living under tons of earth in a structure designed by a layman.

On the aesthetic side, while admitting the difficulty of accounting for tastes, it must also be admitted that too many earth sheltered houses are high on efficiency but low on appearance. If you appreciate quality, the design professional's understanding of scale and form should be just as important to you as his skill with thermal storage and structural stress.

Through a professional, you gain the benefit of current information. It has been said that earth sheltering need not involve any new technologies, just old ones used in new ways. Nevertheless, research, monitoring, and product development continue to provide better insights and techniques. Research papers and new product information are not often addressed to the layperson; the professional you hire should be aware of new developments and able to advise you as to their usefulness.

A final reason for hiring professionals has to do with financing. Lenders have learned through experience that most owner-built houses are poor lending risks. Working with a reputable contractor will actually help in securing a loan; so will your ability to assure the lender that your design either comes from or has been approved by a qualified design professional.

The spectrum of available professional services for earth sheltering is as wide as it is in the conventional building industry. You can hire only design services or only construction services, or find professional service that combines both. The best way to discuss the entire spectrum is to break it into divisions based on your need. In other words, with the exception of specialists like soils engineers and lawyers, the three major types of service providers to consider are those who provide "design only" services, those who provide "design and build" services, and those who provide "build only" services.

Design-Only Services

The Architect as Consultant: What a consulting architect will provide as design services is negotiable but could normally include:

- understanding and developing your program

- checking the site analysis and visiting the site
- preparing preliminary drawings and developing one, through consultation, into an acceptable final design
- preparing construction documents (plans and specifications)

Consulting architectural services on a residence can be and often are even more limited than the above list. The less service you ask for, however, the more responsibility is transferred from the professional to you. The cliché request to "straighten out my design and draw up the construction plans" implies that you take responsibility for the aesthetic and functional aspects of the house. The architect-as-hired-hand is responsible only for your design standing up, staying dry, and meeting codes.

In the real world of residential economics and first-time owner-builders, many suitable homes are developed using only a little consultation with an architect. The more talented and established the architect, however, the less likely he will be interested in helping to fix up a layperson's design.

Architects charge for their services in several ways. For "design only" services, you could arrange for an hourly rate or a flat fee. (What architects traditionally charge when engaged for complete services is discussed later in this section.)

To find an architect who has experience in earth sheltering, consult such national resources as the American Underground-Space Association, the Underground Space Center, and the Conservation and Renewable Energy Inquiry and Referral Service (see Appendix B). Better yet, try your state chapter of the American Institute of Architects or the architecture school at your state university.

Nonprofessional Designers: Since most state laws allow structures under a certain dollar value to be designed by nonprofessionals, many people get into the act of designing homes.

One possible alternative to engaging an architect for consultation, then, is to hire a residence designer. A residence designer will usually modify one of his own or a builder or supplier's stock plans to fit your needs and site. You will receive construction drawings from which a contractor can build the house.

A drafting service is another alternative. Working from your program and perhaps your own sketches, the drafting service draws construction plans that are suitable for securing a building permit or financing. Residence design and drafting services are nearly synonymous; often one individual or firm offers both.

A residence designer or drafting service charges an hourly fee that is less than that of an architect. This kind of designer is a technician rather than a registered professional, and his plans cannot be "stamped" or certified as coming from a registered architect or engineer. Many large cities require such a stamp for any project built within their boundaries, so if you plan to use a residence designer, tell him where you plan to build before you do anything else.

To find a residence designer, look in the Yellow Pages under "Home Designing and Planning Services" or "Drafting Services," call your local or state home-builders' association, or ask a local builder.

Partial or Contributing Designers: Another alternative is to manage the design process yourself but hire specialists for pieces of it, utilizing a drafting service to draw the actual plans. (Even if you are working with an architect, you might find some of these services useful.)

Landscape Architect: For an earth sheltered project, this professional can be helpful in the initial siting and orienting of the house, in planning drainage patterns, in the design of low-maintenance plantings for shallow roof soils, and in locating larger plantings for sun and breeze control. Bringing in a landscape architect at the beginning could be a good investment. To find one with experience or an interest in earth sheltering, call your local or state chapter of the American Society of Landscape Architects or the pertinent school (sometimes architecture, sometimes planning, or a combination) at your state university.

Interior Designer: Like landscape architects, these professionals argue convincingly that their part of the design process for an earth sheltered house is integral, rather than separate. The energy implications of finishing materials are in question, as is the extent to which the inside environment expresses the unique features (warmth, strength, security) of earth sheltering. The time to involve the interior designer and landscape architect may well be during the design process, rather than after it is complete.

Alternative Energy Experts: On a consulting basis, these professionals can be helpful in suggesting and/or evaluating energy-related techniques or materials that are logical in the context of your design and program. To find such experts, call your state energy office and check the literature and periodicals in the library. The commercial field is growing; the Yellow Pages in Minneapolis lists twenty-one firms under the heading "Energy Management and Conservation Consultants"; Salt Lake City lists thirty-nine management firms, plus thirty-three under "Solar Energy Equipment and Systems Dealers" and four under "Windmills."

Mechanical, Electrical, and Structural Engineers: Last on this list of participating designers, engineers are most definitely not the least. Engineers' services are frequently incorporated under the contract with your architect; once the architect has developed the overall plan, the engineer is asked to design the structural, electrical, or mechanical details. In some cases an engineer may have already approved the stock plans you purchase.

Have a structural engineer check self-designed plans before you pile large quantities of earth against walls and roof. An engineer's stamp on plans certifies that, if the structure is built according to the drawings, it will meet the safety requirements of the state. This should add to your peace of mind when you are sitting underneath tons of earth. An engineer's opinion of a layperson's plans is not given lightly. Be prepared to hear that only extensive redesign will satisfy his concerns.

To find these kinds of engineers, call your local Consulting Engineers Council and ask for names of those who have some interest or experience in earth sheltering.

The team approach suggested here is probably most appropriate (and economical) on a project that is larger in scale and budget than a single residence. Furthermore, an architecture firm frequently includes professionals from all of these disciplines. Hiring an architect may land you the entire team in one stroke.

Purchasing Stock Plans: This is probably the least expensive option for "design only" services, but the purchaser of stock or pre-engineered plans should be aware of some hidden costs associated with this option. Buying such a plan will not satisfy your design needs entirely; because of the intimate relationship between an earth sheltered house and its surroundings, someone with the necessary experience should revise or adapt the plans to your site, if not your particular needs.

In addition, many of the stock plans available for earth sheltered houses are not complete construction drawings. You may need additional professional time to convert simple floor plans and elevations into construction documents.

5—2. This house in Massachusetts is an example of a design available as a stock plan from John E. Barnard, Jr., AIA, of Marston Mills, MA. Because of its straight simple lines, this three-bedroom home is not expensive to construct.

SLOPING LOT THREE BEDROOM "ECOLOGY HOUSE"
LIVING AREA   1600
GARAGE   295
JOHN BARNARD JR. A.I.A. OSTERVILLE MA. 02655

DESIGN # S-3BG-A
FLOOR PLAN

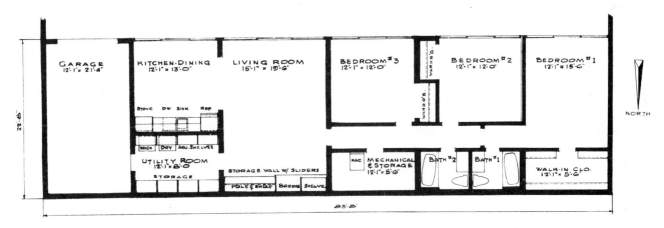

(Drawing courtesy of John Barnard, Jr.)

5–3. Floor plan for the Barnard House shown in figures 5–2 and 5–4. Note that rooms not requiring light and access are ranged along the north, earth-covered wall at the bottom of the drawing.

5–4. Interior view of Barnard's design. For more information on "Ecology House" plans, see Appendix C.

(Photo courtesy of John Barnard, Jr.; reprinted with permission of photographer, Phokion Karas, Medford, MA)

To find books of plans or complete construction documents, see Appendix C.

Design/Build Services

Procuring full-service management for both design and construction can be approached either through an architect or through a builder experienced in earth sheltering.

The Full-Service Architect: You can expect three kinds of basic services from an architect engaged to manage your entire process. First, the architect will assimilate and prepare the elements needed for producing an acceptable design: program, site information, and preliminary drawings.

Second, he will help you find and select a contractor and provide a set of contract documents: detailed plans and specifications that communicate necessary information to the contractor.

Third, the architect will observe the construction for you and advise you of problems. (These basic services are described in greater detail in the next chapter.)

The actual contractual arrangement between owner and architect tends to be fairly informal when the project is not a large, complex building. Other functions may be either included as basic services or provided as additional options. These can include more extensive program development, assistance in site selection, managing a thorough site analysis process, or producing many alternative designs rather than just a few.

Architects commonly use several kinds of fee structures. One traditional method is to charge a percentage of the construction cost. The actual percentage can range from 6 percent of the construction cost for a larger house or a simpler design to 15 percent for a smaller house or a more complicated or detailed one.

Increasingly common is an hourly rate, often with a fixed or estimated maximum specified. Also common is a simple flat fee. For large projects, several methods might be combined: an hourly rate until the basic design is agreed upon, and then, when the scope of the project is thus defined, a flat fee or fixed maximum for the remainder.

Design/Build Architecture Firm: Like the traditional architecture firm, the design/build firm offers a full range of custom-design services, from site information and program development through construction documents. Again, parts of the planning or design process can be purchased as separate consulting services.

The main difference is that the design/build firm offers the client direct construction services as well. Usually by executing a separate and additional contract with you for construction, the firm becomes your general contractor. As such it either uses subcontractors, its own work crews, or a combination of both to build the house.

This combination of custom services is not very common in residential construction, but it is becoming more so. Patterned after the master builders of several centuries ago, the approach has a number of advantages. At least in a small design/build firm, the design architect on a project is likely to be that project's construction manager also. In this way nothing of the intent you agreed on is lost in translation. More important, the design itself is informed by the hands-on field experience the architect has gained in the past or else by the practical knowhow and cost sensitivity of the firm's builder.

If the design/build firm you select has had experience with earth sheltering, your budget will benefit from its skill in product selection and scheduling and from the ability of the project architect to make quick on-site decisions that reflect your preferences. Be sure to agree ahead of time on what kinds of decisions can be made without consultation.

5—5. Schematic drawing of Milo Thompson's design, showing the south elevation from the lake.

(Drawing courtesy of Milo Thompson)

South Elevation

5—6. Milo Thompson, AIA, of Frederick Bentz/Milo Thompson/ Robert Rietow Inc, a Minneapolis architecture and urban design firm, designed this house for a site located on a north woods lake shore. This perspective shows the form of the building.

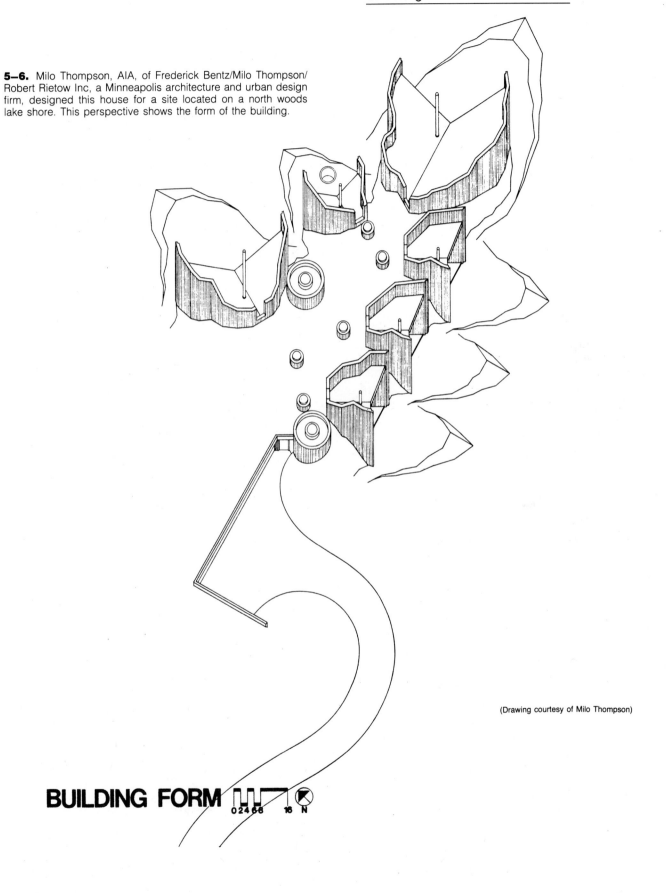

(Drawing courtesy of Milo Thompson)

BUILDING FORM

5—7. The floor plan of the Thompson House shows the spinelike internal circulation plan. Key: 1: Living, 2: Kitchen, 3 & 4: Bedrooms, 5: Bathroom, 6: Master bedroom, 7: Sauna & hot tub.

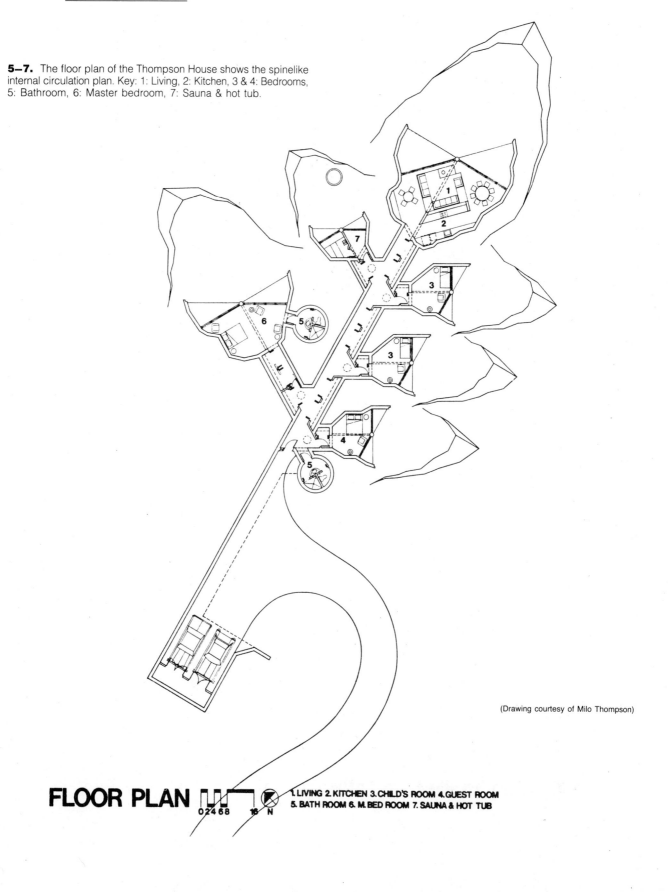

(Drawing courtesy of Milo Thompson)

FLOOR PLAN

0 2 4 6 8   16   N

1. LIVING 2. KITCHEN 3. CHILD'S ROOM 4. GUEST ROOM
5. BATH ROOM 6. M. BED ROOM 7. SAUNA & HOT TUB

(Photo courtesy of Under-the-Earth Homes, Ltd.)

5—8. The south and west walls are exposed on this Wisconsin home designed and built by Under-the-Earth Homes, Ltd., a design/build architecture firm in Cable, WI.

5—9. A view of the Under-the-Earth home's south elevation, showing the attached sunspace.

(Photo courtesy of Under-the-Earth Homes, Ltd.)

Fee structures can vary. A flat fee for the entire package, derived from your project budget, is one alternative. Because of the uncertainties of financing, however, a two-part negotiation for design and construction services might be preferable.

Both of the above alternatives for design/build services are based on the use of registered, professional architects. They share a basic characteristic: they offer a service rather than a known product. You cannot see what you are buying beforehand but must make your selection based on intangibles like personal chemistry, past buildings, and cost estimates. It is worth your while to give some time and care to this selection process.

To find the right architect or design/build firm, use the sources mentioned for consulting architects. Narrow down the choices by paying each candidate a visit. Describe your intended project and note how well you and the architect communicate with one another. Telephone previous clients, look at his portfolio, and visit some of his buildings. Even at this early point, ask for an estimate of how much his services are likely to cost.

The Earth Sheltered Home Builder: If you decide to approach your project with the help of this kind of professional, it will be easier to see what you are buying. The specialized earth sheltered home builder, like traditional home builders, usually works from a selection of predesigned plans. Over the past several years, a number of earth sheltered construction companies have emerged. Some have developed particular building systems that allow them to build your earth sheltered home quite inexpensively and quickly.

Earth sheltered building companies ordinarily provide the consumer with reliable, well-tested designs whose details have been perfected through experience. The advantage they offer, in addition to their practical experience and skill, is that the plans they provide are already engineered for safety and reliability. (If they are not engineered, find another source for your plans.) Using a national company that transports its own crews to your site for critical parts of the construction is also a good strategy if you have not been able to find local experienced builders.

The disadvantages are that your design is not specifically tailored to your situation; it may in fact be overengineered because it must be reliable under varying conditions. Also, of course, your design options are more limited. You get what is offered rather than specifically what you want.

5—10. An Earth Shelter Corporation house in Hamilton, MA. Both this and the Barrington house are models, open to the public.

5–11. An earth sheltered house built in Barrington, IL, to standard plans by Earth Shelter Corporation of America, Berlin, WI. The design features a small, conventionally built aboveground level. The exterior rolling shutters on the windows are closed in the evening.

5–12. A close-up of the south elevation of the Barrington house:

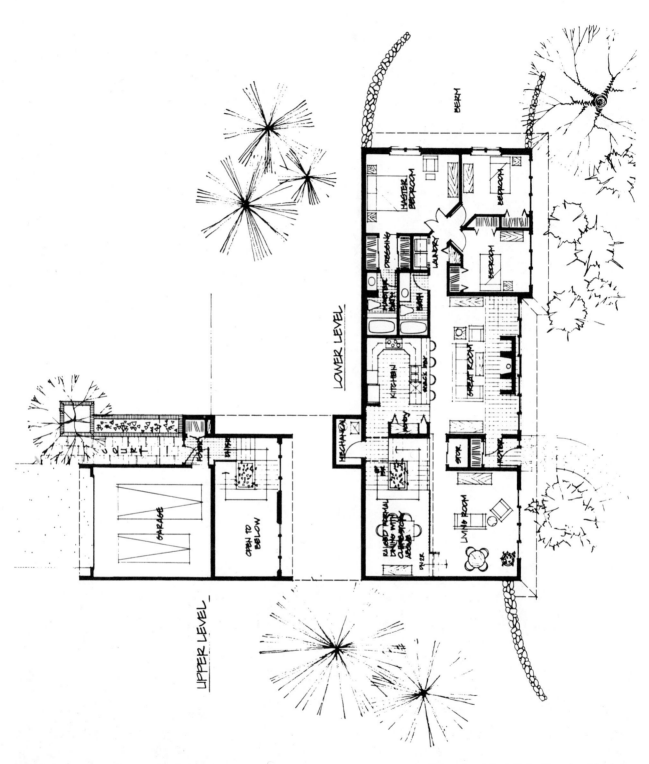

5—13. Floor plan for the Hamilton house. The upper level's aboveground garage/back entry makes the house look more conventional and also provides more light to the dining and living areas.

(Copyright 1982, Earth Shelter Corporation of America)

Selecting the Professionals

List your potential candidates, saving contractor selection until after design. Start with a telephone survey to narrow down your choices, using the worksheet to keep track of your reactions to each contact. Make your final selection by paying personal visits both to your candidates' offices and to buildings they have designed or built.

	Candidate A	Candidate B
Name/Address/Phone		
Interest or experience in earth sheltering		
Personal comments		
Fee		
References		

To find such a builder, call your local home-builders' association, check the Yellow Pages, or consult Appendix C at the back of this book.

Build-Only Services

The General Contractor: Even though you pay the extra costs of overhead and profit, hiring a contractor is usually preferable to being your own general contractor. The time you will save in scheduling and record keeping alone will make the extra cost worthwhile. Actual selection of a contractor cannot take place until you have a set of plans and specifications from which he can make a construction bid. Therefore, a more complete discussion of locating and selecting a contractor is presented in chapter 7, *Preparing to Build*.

At this point, if you have completed all the tasks and activities suggested from the beginning of this book, you are roughly at the stage where most people begin. Even though your work from now on will be shared by a professional, you have done sufficient predesign planning on your own to create a basis of knowledge that will immeasurably improve the results of the partnership you are now beginning.

You have been continually evaluating the appropriateness of earth sheltering for your climate, location, site, and resources. Most important, you have pinpointed your personal needs, goals, and resources. Watching the fruits of your preliminary efforts take shape in the form of an actual design should now be enormously satisfying.

Chapter 6

The Design Process

A design for a house is the result of a creative process that may be rather mysterious to laypeople. Discovering how an architect organizes the progressive stages of design may demystify the process somewhat.

Why an Architect?

Designing a good house is a challenge; designing an earth sheltered house that works well is an even greater one. Such a house is so intimately related to its particular microclimate and site that no set of rules or statements about what kind of design is successful or appropriate can be all-encompassing.

What would work in Missouri may not in Colorado, so if a good and appropriate design is important to you, then invest in the judgment, experience, and creativity of an architect.

A common perception of the architect's job is that he or she can and will simply take the owner's design and fix it up. By suggesting in this book that you try your own hand at arranging spaces and even produce some drawings, we are seemingly reinforcing the idea that you should hire an architect to start in the middle of the process. On the contrary, we think you will find that the architect will be interested in your ideas, but that you will not be taking the best advantage of his skill to approach him only for polishing up your own design.

Owner-Architect Responsibilities

Owner and architect share the responsibility to develop together the analysis necessary to begin the design. It is up to the owner to provide personal and site information through a program that is as concise as possible. It is the architect's task to probe, understand, develop, and especially with regard to the site, to verify the owner's information.

Extensive site analysis is not part of the basic services an architect normally provides. Though he may arrange, direct, and interpret the results of soil borings and surveys, the owner will pay for them.

The architect will visit your site, of course, as part of his responsibility for predesign information. His visit will help him determine the best spot and orientation for the house. He may charge extra for an elaborate process of site evaluation and planning so you should develop as much site information as possible on your own.

The architect must also be familiar with applicable codes and ordinances. In fact, as a registered practitioner, he has a responsibility to protect the public's safety, health, and welfare by avoiding unsound design or practice; knowledge of standards and codes are tools of his trade.

Financial responsibilities are divided. Of course, it is your responsibility to secure the financing for the project and to pay the architect. His responsibility is to provide you with a reliable estimate of his own design fee, as well as increasingly accurate estimates of construction costs as you progress through each stage of design.

Finally, the architect is responsible for several kinds of drawings to communicate the design: schematic or sketchlike renditions that provide your first opportunity for assessment; increasingly detailed and technical drawings as the design is developed; and finally the specific documents from which the builder can work.

Stages of Design

Program Evaluation and Development
Although the sequence of increasingly detailed drawings defines individual design steps, the process actually begins not with drawings but with your program. At this stage, communication is between owner and the architect. Its purpose is to define the personal and site elements that will influence the design and to identify any internal contradictions these elements pose. At the end of this stage, any estimate the architect can make of the cost of construction is likely to be accurate only to within about 25 percent.

Schematic Design
The birth of the design idea is really the heart of the mystery. The architect, working alone, produces the rough sketches that give the first form to the building. The beginning sketches are, of course, very personal; these are communications between the architect and himself. Working from your program, he locates spaces in relation to one another and gives them size and proportion. Rooms or areas of activity first appear as sketchy circles (the "bubbles"), which he keeps rearranging until their relationships work.

The result of this process is a set of drawings called schematic drawings. They are intended solely for communicating the design idea to the owner. For this reason they are very pictorial: nearly the equivalent of photographs.

Several kinds of schematic drawings help explain the design to the owner. First, there may be a *site plan*. Unlike the site map you prepared before, the architect's site plan will show the house as it will be placed on the lot (see fig. 6-1).

There will be floor plans for each level and a set of *elevations*. An elevation in this case is a drawing of the proposed building from the outside; each elevation will show a separate face of the building.

Elevations are not as descriptive of earth sheltered buildings as they are when they can show the exposed walls of an aboveground house. Therefore, schematics may also include other kinds of renderings to help you understand the designer's idea. *Perspectives* show the building in three dimensions from various angles. *Sections* are useful for communicating interior room shapes and heights and their relation to the outside; instead of showing the interior from above, as the floor plan does, a section shows the inside as though the building had been sliced open from top to bottom.

The schematic drawings may also include a written outline, much abbreviated, of the materials specifications. For example, the architect may specify concrete construction, but whether it will be block, precast, or poured-in-place is left to be decided in the next stage. Keep in mind, however, that the choice of design will partly determine the choice of materials.

Cost estimates from the schematic drawings are likely to be accurate to within 15 to 20 percent.

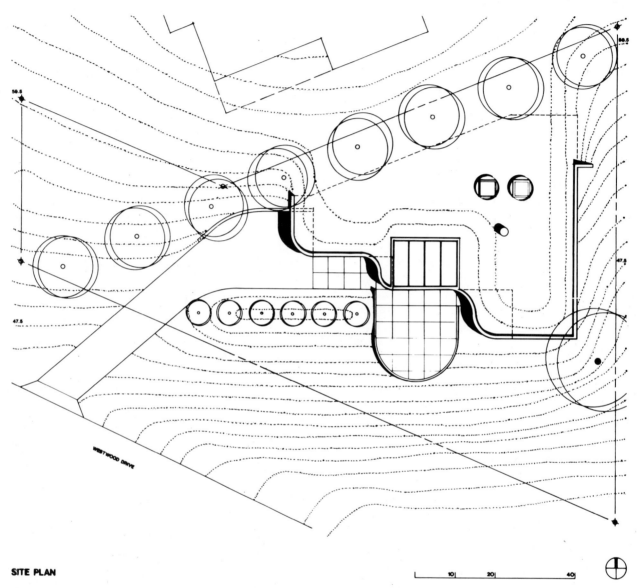

SITE PLAN

6–1. An example of a site plan for an urban location. This is the site plan of the Chilless house shown in figures 2–24, 2–25, 2–26, and 2–27.

(Drawing courtesy of Tedd Chilless)

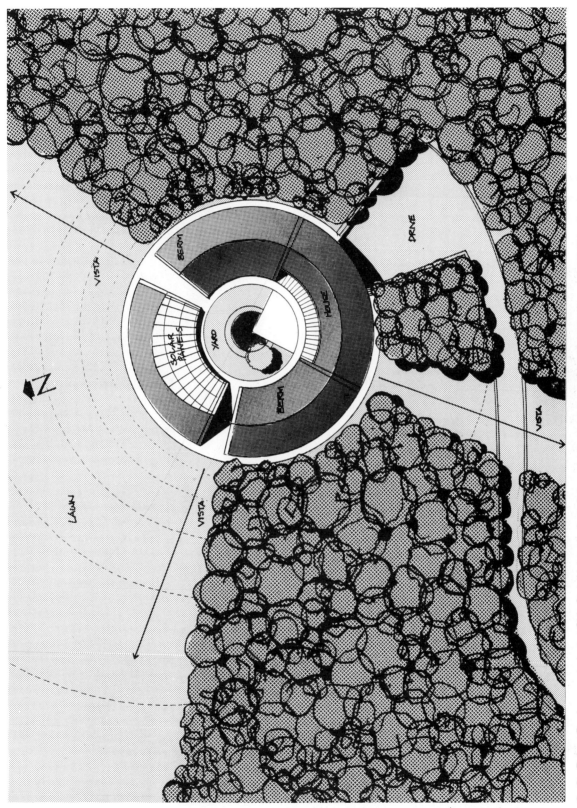

6–2. Robert Banbury, a student at Ohio State University, entered this design for a house in a circular berm in AUA's 1981 Design Competition. Openings in the berm separate the solar collection system and its gadgetry from the house itself. This site plan shows the ground sloping down towards the north, with the house sited at the edge of woods at the top of the slope.

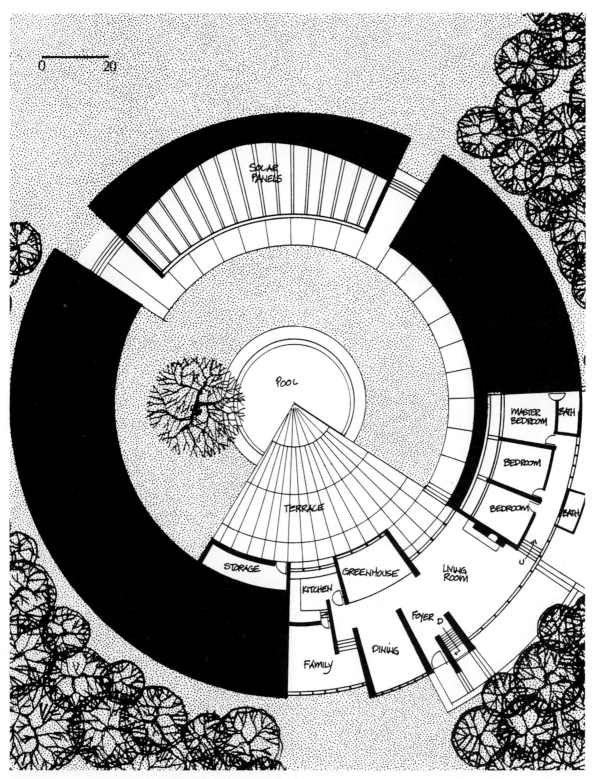

6—3. The main level floor plan of the Banbury house shows, as the designer explains, a "modified American Ranch" layout. A lower level below the bedrooms contains garage, workshop and laundry.

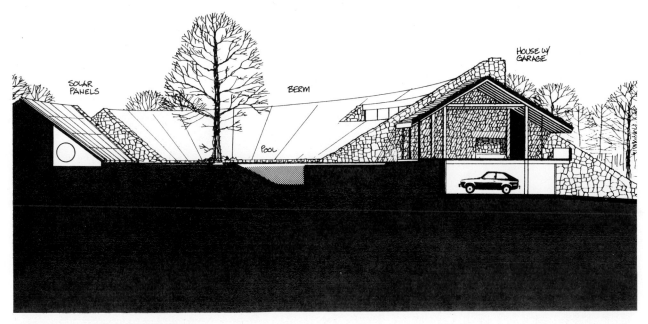

6—4. A section of the Banbury house.

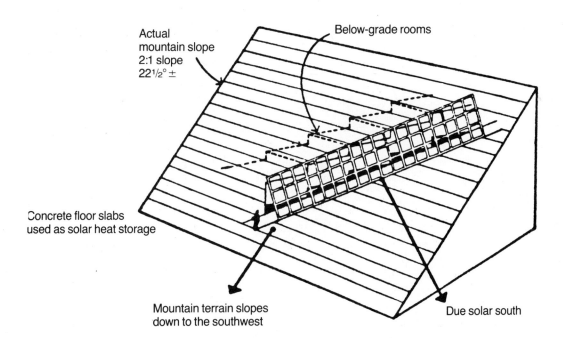

Actual
mountain slope
2:1 slope
22½° ±

Below-grade rooms

Concrete floor slabs
used as solar heat storage

Mountain terrain slopes
down to the southwest

Due solar south

(Drawing courtesy of Robert Hull)

6—5. Though not technically a site plan, this drawing helps explain how the concept for a lovely house in Washington developed out of a difficult site constraint. Robert Hull of Miller/Hull Partnership, Seattle, WA, solved the problem of a steep southwesterly slope by skewing the house and its solar collector window wall up the mountain. Result: the collector faces due south, the incline's steepness is reduced to a walkable ramp, and ramp and collector combine to become the structure's internal circulation path.

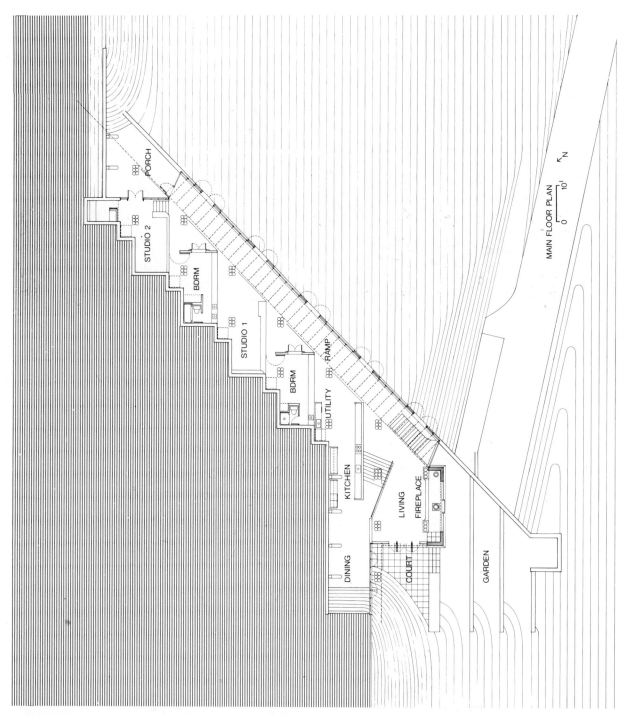

6—6. The floor plan for the main level of the Hull house. Under the garden and living room is a garage and an under-slab rock bin that stores heat ducted from the top of the window wall collector.

(Drawing courtesy of Robert Hull)

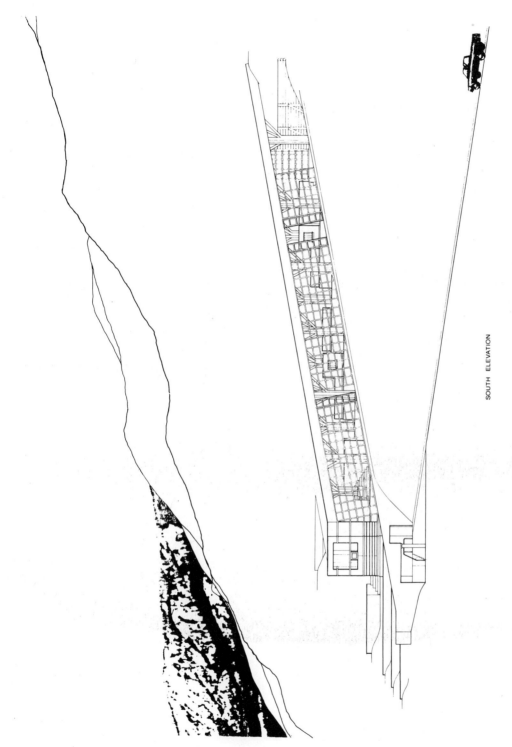

SOUTH ELEVATION

6—7. An elevation of the Hull house. Because perspective is not used in an elevation, faces of the building not perpendicular to the viewer look misshapen.

(Drawing courtesy of Robert Hull)

AXONOMETRIC

(Drawing courtesy of Robert Hull)

6—8. A perspective demonstrates the concept of the Hull house perhaps best of all. This shows the stepped levels for each room rising up the incline and the supporting treelike wood columns that suggest a northwest "lodge" house.

Personal Schematic Designs

Try your hand at a few schematic designs. Get out your site map and locate the best position for your house based on slope orientation, soil conditions, and views. Working from the "bubble" drawings you experimented with in chapter 5, try out some floor plans and elevations. Locate doors and windows, keeping in mind such considerations as light, access to the outside, and internal circulation.

Personal schematic designs

Design Assessment

The purpose of the schematic design drawings is to define the scope and idea of the house. They are the realization of your program in the shape of an actual building, but they are really only a beginning. The more arduous task of arriving at complete, construction-ready drawings will begin as soon as your reaction to the schematic design is communicated.

The most appropriate criteria for owner assessment of the design are personal ones. Unless you are also a skilled and experienced designer or builder, a technical evaluation is probably not feasible. Therefore, although you should raise lots of questions about technical points, keep your actual evaluation on safe ground by comparing it to your program.

To ask intelligent questions and understand the trade-offs inherent in any design, you probably need more familiarity with earth sheltered building materials and processes than heretofore provided. More description of these items is in the discussion of actual construction in chapter 9.

The first criterion for your evaluation should be the relationship of the proposed building to the site. Questions to ask yourself might be:

● Do the form and proportion appear to fit the site comfortably? Are the views—of the building

Building a Model

The architect can make a scale model of the design for you, but we recommend that you do it yourself. You will learn much about the proposed building this way. Use ⅛- to ¼-inch foam core board, a lightweight board with a foam center faced on both sides with white paper. It is easy to cut and available under various brand names at art-supply stores. Working from the schematic drawings, cut the pieces of foam core to scale and include retaining walls, windows, doors, and other details.

Model makers generally use hot melt glue to hold sections together. Glue pellets and the heating gun are available at hardware stores; hot glue is laid down in a bead that sets quickly, making it a better choice than white glue, which requires holding or clamping until the glue sets.

The model is a tangible vehicle for assessing the design. Take it to the site at various times of day and watch where the sun falls. Make cutouts to scale of any large pieces of furniture to see if they will fit. Look into windows through a straw and imagine yourself walking through hallways, opening doors, and working in the kitchen.

6—9. Robert Hull's model for the mountain house illustrated in figures 6–6, 6–7, and 6–8, showing the value of a removable roof for viewing the interior.

(Photo courtesy of Robert Hull)

from a distance, through the windows to the outside—pleasant?
- Will the orientation, placement, and protection of windows and doors take maximum advantage of sunlight and prevailing breezes?
- Are potential surface and subsurface drainage problems addressed?
- Will the house conform to codes and zoning ordinances and be compatible with the neighborhood?

The next set of criteria are specific to the your goals and preferences regarding performance, design, and room list. In addition to checking the design against these program items, ask yourself:

- Are the traffic patterns well thought out?
- Do the building materials implied in the design suit my tastes, maintenance skills, and budget?
- Are the indoor/outdoor transitions handled satisfactorily?

How well the design fits your personal resources is the remaining consideration. The construction cost estimate plus 20 percent should be comfortably within your project budget, because design fees, contingencies, and various smaller fees must also be included in the total. Ask yourself:

- Can I afford this design?
- Am I capable of doing any part of the construction or finishing myself?

Written Assessment of Schematic Design

Make notes of your assessments of the design, using the wish lists and goals statements in your program as guides for organizing your comments. Consider the questions posed and add your own.

It is not necessary to be formal, because your reactions should be communicated verbally as well as in written form.

● Site Comments: _____
_____
_____

● Personal Comments:

What the house should do (performance goals):

Goal	Comment

What the house should look like (design goals):

Goal	Comment

The kinds of rooms I want:

Type of Room	Comments on characteristics (size, shape)
Working rooms	
Living rooms	
Sleeping rooms	

Comments on room arrangements: _____
_____
_____

The ideas shaped in schematic drawings may be what you asked for but still unsatisfactory. Before requesting a whole new approach, rethink your program. Unnoticed inconsistencies are most likely to crop up now, given form by an actual design. This situation is not uncommon and can never be dealt with more effectively than now. Decide which of your preferences should be sacrificed and send the architect back to the drawing board.

A caution, however: if you are still not satisfied after having seen two or even three alternative designs that are not just refinements but whole new approaches, then you should consider paying the necessary portion of the design fee, hiring a different architect, and beginning again.

Design Development

The purpose of this stage is to define the building in total. It begins with the owner communicating to the architect his assessment of the schematic design.

Working together, owner and architect identify

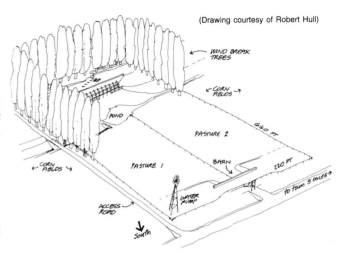

(Drawing courtesy of Robert Hull)

6–10. The site plan for a farmhouse in Washington. Like the mountain house in figures 6–5 through 6–9, this variation of an elevational style home is by Robert Hull, Seattle, WA. A harsh climate and the family's interest in energy self-sufficiency suggest a passive solar earth sheltered design on this nearly flat site.

6–11. The Hull farm house floor plan shows house functions slanted to allow space for a centrally focused greenhouse. The dotted line indicates the actual roof line. The on-grade entry is tunnellike, penetrating the berm on the north side.

(Drawing courtesy of Robert Hull)

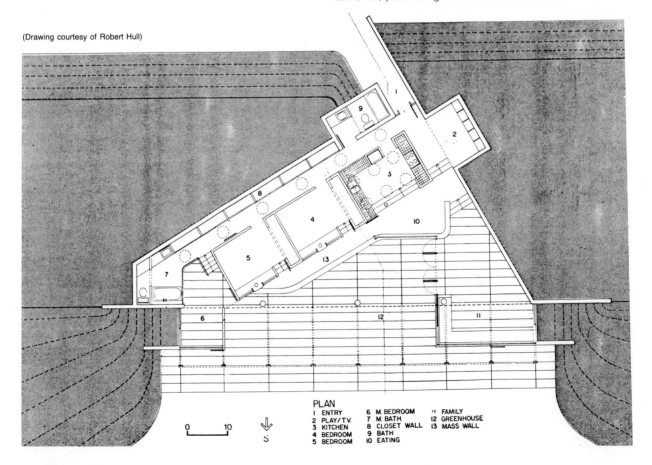

PLAN
1	ENTRY	6 M. BEDROOM	11 FAMILY
2	PLAY/T.V.	7 M. BATH	12 GREENHOUSE
3	KITCHEN	8 CLOSET WALL	13 MASS WALL
4	BEDROOM	9 BATH	
5	BEDROOM	10 EATING	

0   10

6—12. Two perspectives show the Hull farmhouse with roof and earth cover and without. In the "roof on" perspective, the greenhouse is shown in summer mode: a fixed, slanted, double-glazed greenhouse roof is topped with horizontal louvered shading. The shading clips on to residential garage doors that roll down on the tracks to enclose the greenhouse in winter. Two of the doors are shown at right in winter position.

(Drawing courtesy of Robert Hull)

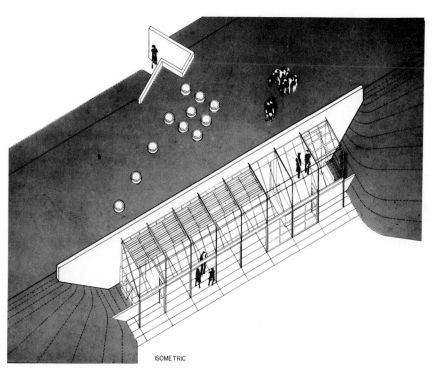

ISOMETRIC

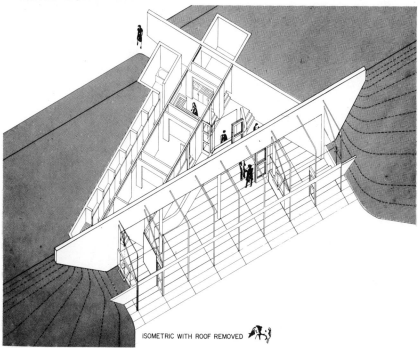

ISOMETRIC WITH ROOF REMOVED

specifically the house's characteristics and materials. For example, schematic drawings may show eight rooms of certain sizes and shapes; developing the room designs now includes locating electric outlets, deciding where bookshelves go and what kind of windows are wanted. How the roof will be con-

structed, what specific kinds of building materials, waterproofing products, and drainage devices will be used, how the efficiency of heating and cooling systems can be maximized, what the landscape plan will include—these and other such specific and technical decisions are all made at this stage. Many

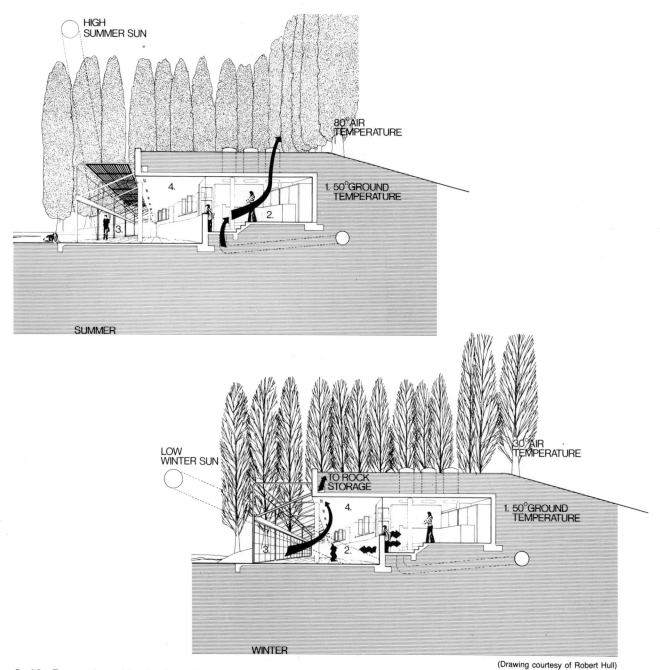

(Drawing courtesy of Robert Hull)

6–13. Two sections of the farmhouse illustrate the interior spaces as well as the role played by the "variable skin" in the energy plan for summer and winter. The solution to the summer overheating tendencies of a greenhouse was to simply take it away by means of the roll-up glazed garage doors.

changes in the design will result as these issues are considered and resolved.

This is the point at which the architect should be carefully questioned about the implications of the energy-related mechanical systems that may have been incorporated into the design. For example:

- What guarantee is there that this solar hot water heater or heat pump really works?
- How much energy will it save? At what cost?
- What testing has been done?
- If it breaks down, what kind of service is available for repairing this type of equipment?

During the design development process, the drawings become more and more technical and the specifications more detailed. Pay close attention and ask many questions, because this period holds the greatest potential for self-education. When construction actually begins, your ability to monitor it intelligently will depend on your familiarity with the plans and specifications and your consequent understanding of the components, details, and trade-offs represented in the final design.

Contract Documents

In this stage the pattern of the communication shifts. No longer between owner and architect, the communication is now between the owner/architect "group" and the (currently hypothetical) contractor.

The communication is in the form of contract documents; that is, the written materials embodying the contract that will bind the builder (the "contractor") to produce the building as designed. Contract documents include two different types of communication. There are detailed plans (floor plans, elevations, sections, drawings of structural, mechanical, and electrical details) and a book of specifications includes lists of materials, dates when construction should start and finish, and other instructions necessary for contractors to make informed bids.

These documents have three purposes. The first is to inform the contractor about the building. The second is to provide a basis for a price. Since items like doorknobs, wires, and amounts of lumber or concrete can now be counted, the final estimate in the form of a contractor's bid can now be made. (The bidding process is described more fully in the next chapter.) The third purpose of the documents is to form part of the actual contract between owner and contractor. *It is binding:* if the resulting building is not the one described in contract documents, the owner can withhold payment.

Should a failure occur after construction, the contract documents are the legal evidence for assigning liability. If they show a design error, the liability is the architect's. If failure results from the contractor not following the design (less reinforcing steel than was specified, for example), then the contractor is liable.

Although detailed plans and specifications are not always done for a house, request them for an earth sheltered house. For instance, make sure the architect specifies not only the waterproofing and insulating materials to be used, but also the application process, including acceptable weather conditions and timing. The contractor should understand those specific conditions and accept liability if his crew's performance does not conform.

Make sure landscaping is included in the plans and specifications. The surface contouring, retaining walls, soils, and plantings are an integral part of your design, not a cosmetic addition tacked on later when you can afford them. Their presence in contract documents ensures their cost will be included in the contractor's bid.

Drawing and/or describing every detail in contract documents is expensive but well worth doing to prevent misunderstandings later. Here, however, the value of experienced earth sheltered builders is further revealed: if the architect does not need to produce construction drawings that are complete in every detail, everyone saves money.

In preparing specifications and final drawings, the architect ordinarily supplements his own expertise with that of an engineer and one or more suppliers. The specific structural, mechanical, and electrical design work will be referred to an engineer; the specifics for precast concrete planks, for example, may be left to a supplier. The supplier returns "shop drawings" to the architect that specify the amount, size, and lengths of planks that will be provided to satisfy the design. It is the architect's responsibility to make sure the shop drawings specify the correct materials prior to signing them.

When the architect has completed the contract documents, the construction cost estimate he can produce should be accurate to within 10 to 15 percent. The contractor's bid, when received, will further define the construction cost. As the next chapter shows, once you have a bid, you can check it against your original project budget.

Chapter 7

Preparing to Build

In this intermediate stage, a number of things that could not be done without a design must be accomplished—and seemingly all at once. Before you are even ready to seek financing, you will need the plans and specifications, and the help of your architect, to complete the tasks described in this chapter.

Selecting the Right Contractor

We begin from the premise that it is not economical to be your own general contractor on an earth sheltered project unless you have previous experience. Scheduling is complex: timing, for example, can mean the difference between successful application of the waterproofing/insulation systems and complete failure caused by exposure to the elements. It is much smarter to choose an experienced contractor who is able to handle subcontractors, analyze their bids, evaluate their performance, and manipulate the complex scheduling for a smooth flow of work.

If you decided to purchase combined design and construction services, your contractor is auto-matically chosen along with design or designer. If you are working with an architect or have purchased stock plans, your search for a builder can now begin.

A good contractor can build a good building from a poor set of drawings. Even a good set of drawings, however, cannot make an incompetent contractor look good. In other words, choosing a contractor is, next to your choice of designer, the most important decision you will make.

You will be fortunate to find a competent builder who also has earth sheltered experience. More likely, you will be interviewing builders with little or no earth sheltered experience, and you will have to make an educated guess as to which one will perform best. Be prepared to spend time on this step, because again you are buying an unknown service rather than a tangible product.

Not only will your contractor's performance be critical to the success of the project; almost as important, his reputation may actually help you secure a loan. A lender will underwrite an innovative project more readily if the builder involved has a good track record for integrity and thoroughness.

You can expect to select a smaller contracting

Surveying Contractors

To reduce your list of potential contractors, either your own finds or those recommended by your architect, make a telephone survey. Briefly describe your project to each contractor, giving the location and schedule. Ask each interested contractor the list of questions shown on the worksheet. Pay particular attention to how well you communicate with one another.

Name			
Address/Phone			
State/Local license number			
Are you bonded?			
Do you: offer guarantees/warranties?			
have insurance: liability, theft?			
work on-site or only visit?			
How long in business?			
How many homes have you built?			
How many earth sheltered homes?			
What price range do you build in?			
Affiliations:			
Communication potential:			
Interest in project:			
Willingness to bid:			
References:			

firm, as most large residential contractors are accustomed to building houses that are not one of a kind. Specialized or experienced earth sheltered contractors, like most custom builders who will be interested in your project, probably build only a few houses at a time. Since you will want to work very closely with the contractor, the kind of personal relationship possible with a small firm will be to your benefit.

Locating Candidates

To find appropriate contractors to consider, start

with your architect's recommendations. He will know who most of the local contractors are, how they tend to bid a project, and what kind of work they do.

If you are not working with an architect, identify candidates by calling your local or state homebuilders' association, Association of General Contractors, Poured Wall Contractors' Association, or materials supplier. Do not neglect the Yellow Pages. If you live in a metropolitan area, you might also list your project with the Builders' Exchange, a periodically updated listing of projects out for bid. A Builders' Exchange is a way for contractors to find out about upcoming jobs.

Do not necessarily limit your search to contractors in the immediate vicinity, but remember that the closer your site is to his office or home, the more frequent the contractor's supervision and inspection trips can be.

Once your list is of manageable length, reduce it further by calling former clients of each builder. Visit a few of your candidates' houses, especially observing the work crews at any that are currently under construction.

Finally, you will want to know if the contractor is financially stable and will be around to back up his work. This may be self-evident for a large, old firm, but it is a significant issue for the small or new company. Ask for and check references, check Dun & Bradstreet (though a small outfit may not be listed), and call the Better Business Bureau.

Making your final selection can be done either through competitive bidding or through negotiation.

The Bidding Process

The advantage of this method is that you are able to assess the abilities and estimates of several contractors by comparing their bids, the speed with which they think they can complete your project, and the amount of overhead and profit each will charge. Since bids will be made on the basis of your contract documents, these documents should include instructions to bidders, specifying such terms and conditions as when you want the bid, how you want it itemized, bonding requirements, and target start and finish dates.

Conditions that are too stringent will discourage builders who would naturally prefer single negotiation to the risk of investing time in an unsuccessful bid. Nevertheless, you should ask that the bids show both the costs for time and materials of specific parts of the job and also the percentage used to calculate overhead and profit.

The bids are fixed; that is, they represent a not to be exceeded contract price. The contractor himself must pay any additional costs beyond this amount. By the same token, he pockets the difference if the costs are less than his fixed bid. Change orders during the course of construction are actual changes in the contract, legitimately resulting in modifications to the fixed bid price.

The bids are all opened at the same time, possibly with the architect assisting in tabulation. Contractors may be present during the opening of bids.

Evaluating Bids and Bidders: You are not bound to take the lowest bid. Explore with lower bidders the possibility that minor extras are not being included in the figures. It is frustrating to be charged extra for the light bulbs when the cost for the fixture was itemized and you assumed they would be included. Usually these details are not actually specified in the contract for a residential project.

Evaluating the contractor's ability and experience in reading plans will teach you a lot about his flexibility and competence. Sit down with each final candidate and spread your plans out. If the contractor is used to working in wood and your plans specify reinforced concrete, they may look more like drawings for the space shuttle than house plans to him. Ask him to tell you about your plans; look for a person who is willing to study them seriously—and *use* them!

Ask specific questions related to your particular project that might demonstrate the contractor's earth sheltered expertise or ability to solve problems. For example:

- What building sequence would you use?
- I have a two-way floor slab; how do you pour that differently from a one-way slab?
- What do you normally do to achieve a good airless pour?
- How would you handle the backfilling?

Slip in a few trick questions that any good contractor should be able to spot as a wrong assumption or else be straightforward about confessing ignorance. Innocently pose one of these:

- Are you going to use aluminum conduit? (never used in concrete)
- How much salt do you allow in the concrete—20 percent? (rarely over 2 percent)

Your architect can help develop more project specific questions and interpret the answers.

The Negotiation Process

This is an alternative selection process often used in residential projects. It has several advantages over the bidding process. By working out the price with a single contractor, you may save some money because your contract documents can be abbreviated. If time is at a premium, the negotiation process is the preferable alternative because it is shorter. Finally, the process works better in the case of a project with many factors that cannot be fully known at the time of bidding. When that large boulder or torrential rainstorm increases the amount of excavation work, for example, you can rest easier knowing there is a prearranged formula for covering extra costs.

Negotiations can be organized in several ways. You can start with several candidate contractors, asking each to supply a bid specifying only the overhead and profit he will charge. (The assumption here is that the other factors in an estimate, time and materials, are likely to be similar among all potential bidders.) A final choice can be made based on the variable overhead and profit factors.

Negotiation with a single contractor avoids any semblance of a competitive bidding process. Perhaps you already know the contractor with whom you wish to work because of his admirable work for a friend, the amount of free advice he may already have given you, or his experience in earth sheltering. You may not pay any more by using a negotiation process, and you might offend a builder with whom you already have some relationship by asking him to go back through a time-consuming formal bidding process.

A negotiation, unlike a fixed bid process, does not necessarily imply that there will be a not to be exceeded cost. Your negotiation should include such a limit, together with provisions for the disposition of remaining amounts if the maximum cost is not reached, as well as a provision for change orders. A negotiating process is not undertaken with more than one contractor at a time. In general, profit margins and overhead are the items that are negotiated.

Upon selection of a contractor, ask that the final itemized bid, whether arrived at by competitive bidding or negotiation, be signed and certified by the contractor. Lenders often ask that this sworn construction statement accompany the loan application. The itemized bid should be accurate to within 5 percent of the actual cost, although a 10 percent leeway is usually allowed.

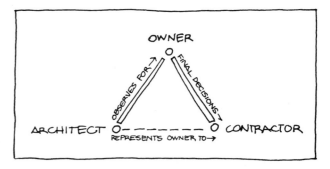

7–1. The architect/owner/contractor relationship.

The Contract

As stated in chapter 6, the architect's plans and specifications comprise the bulk of the owner/contractor agreement. Obviously, the more specific they are, the less room there is for future misunderstandings about who is responsible for unforeseen costs—the owner or the contractor. If you are using stock plans, be sure all addenda to the plans are attached in writing *prior* to the bidding process so all material costs can be included in the original bids.

Under no circumstances is it economical to build without working drawings or specifications. With nothing in writing, you as an owner would be extremely vulnerable to the possibility that the contractor will interpret further details as additions—a costly battle for both owner and contractor.

It is worthwhile to employ an attorney to draw up or review the building contract for your home. He or she is obligated to represent your interests and that protection can be invaluable. In addition to the plans and specifications, which become a part of the agreement, consider including the following points.

Architect/Owner/Contractor Relationship: Generally this relationship is like a triangle. That is, the architect observes construction on behalf of the owner and represents the owner's interests with the contractor. All final decisions must go through the owner rather than directly between the architect and contractor.

This basic formula can vary according to the owner's wishes, however, so specify in the contract the pattern of decision making you wish. For instance, the owner could say, "The architect is authorized to act on my behalf in all things; therefore, Mr. Contractor, discuss everything with my architect as he has final say" or "I, the owner, will observe construction myself and carry on all negotiations directly with the contractor."

(Photo courtesy of John Barnard; reprinted with permission of photographer Phokion Karas, Medford, MA)

7–2. The east elevation of an atrium house in Stow, MA, designed by John Barnard, Jr., AIA.

Start-up: The start-up date and agreed upon completion date should be included in the contract. (The dates, as indeed the entire contract, are likely to have to be contingent on the owner's securing of financing.) Any penalties associated with late completion must also be in writing.

Warranty: Ask for a one-year warranty on the house and workmanship, with the contractor responsible for repairing defects. Guarantees of separately installed equipment (mechanical systems, movable window insulation) are between owner and supplier, and the contractor should be separated from liability in the contract.

Changes/Substitutions: Changes to the plans or specifications (for instance, the substitution of one material for another) should take place only with mutual consent.

A change order is used to alter or amend the contract when a change in cost will result. Change orders use standard forms that both architects and contractors have on hand. Generally the architect

has responsibility for a change order but would inform the owner before signing it. You may wish to specify in the contract that you will sign all change orders. Minor changes that do not result in significant cost changes are handled through simple verbal negotiation.

Contingencies: Carefully consider any contingencies the contractor wants included in the contract. Under a "lump sum" or fixed bid, the contractor is responsible for any additional costs caused by any problem not specifically mentioned in the contract. The contractor may want additional costs resulting from "Acts of God" to be negotiated and may also try to include strikes or weather delays as contingencies.

The lump sum contract is the owner's all-risk protection policy; do not give up the protection a fixed price offers against unforeseen extra costs without getting something in return. For example, when contingencies are specified, the party responsible for payment, should the contingency arise, is negotiable. If the contractor wants to name many contingencies, he may be satisfied with a lower profit margin in return.

Cost Overruns: Make sure it is clear who is responsible for paying for cost overruns—the contractor or the owner. A "fudge factor" of perhaps 10 percent might already have been included by the contractor in his fixed bid. This is a perfectly legitimate practice but may or may not be obvious in the itemized bid. Feel free to ask the contractor: if a fudge factor is included, any overrun should be understood to be his responsibility.

Permits: The contractor should be responsible for securing and paying for all building permits unless the contract specifically exempts him from this duty.

Cleanup: Include cleanup in the contract if you do not care to do it yourself or find cheaper labor for the job. At a minimum the site should be picked up, the house floors swept, and dripped paint removed from windows and other visible surfaces.

Insurance: Both the owner and the contractor should be required in writing to contribute to the insurance for the project. In general, it is the contractor's responsibility to provide the liability coverage, and yours to provide the insurance to protect the property during construction. Usually an extension of your current homeowner's policy will be sufficient until you move in and begin a new policy.

Computing Total Project Costs

List the expenses or estimates of expenses asked for on the work sheet. Not all of them can be included in your financing, but the total they represent is an important figure to compare against your original project budget.

Design fees	$_____
Construction cost (plus 10% for contingencies)	_____
Separate fees not included in the above, such as:	
legal fees	_____
soils tests	_____
surveys	_____
permit fees*	_____
utility connection fees*	_____
appraisal, other financing fees*	_____
insurance costs	_____
landscaping fees	_____
interior decorating fees	_____
moving costs	_____
Furniture	_____
Equipment	_____
Land costs, if not already owned	_____
Total	$_____

*Estimated amounts of these fees appear later in this chapter and the next.

Finishing Work: If the owner is doing any finishing work, *specifically* exclude that from the contract work.

Price and Manner of Payment: Payment usually takes place in installments based on satisfactory completion of work. The payment schedule could reflect completion of the most significant intermediate steps in an earth sheltered project: the rough shell, the exterior finishing (waterproofing, insulating, and backfill), and interior finishing. Frequently 10 percent of payment is withheld until the owner's final approval is given.

Reassessing the Cost

Total Costs

With the contractor's bid in hand, you are now in a position to know, within about 10 percent, what

the whole project will cost. Before you submit plans to a building code official or apply for a mortgage, total all your costs to make sure they fit your budget.

Energy Costs

Assuming that one of your main reasons for choosing the earth sheltered alternative is its energy economy, you should now make an attempt to assess how cost-effective your design choices really are. For add-on features like a solar hot water heater, you can be fairly precise about specific savings and evaluate the investment accordingly.

Most of the energy-saving features of an earth sheltered house, however, are also structural: they are not just part of the house, they *are* the house. Removing them is a question of redesigning the building. Earth on the roof, for example, increases the structural cost by requiring larger footings, stronger walls, and higher-quality waterproofing.

Computing Energy Costs and Savings

The following exercise should help you think through the implications of your design choice. The computations probably cannot be specific enough to distinguish the extra costs of specific structural design features, but forcing yourself and your designer to confront the issue of energy cost-effectiveness may produce a more carefully considered design.

Anticipated Additional Building Costs

1. *Energy Saving Features:* List both structural items like earth on the roof or an insulated floor slab, and add-on features like solar collectors or night window insulation. With the help of your contractor, calculate the added costs these features represent.

Feature	Description	Added Cost
1.		$
2.		$
3.		$
Total extra cost		

2. *Energy Investment:*

Total anticipated extra building cost		Energy tax credits (state energy office)		Front-end energy investment
$_____	−	$_____	=	$_____

Anticipated Energy Savings

1. *Anticipated yearly energy use in Btu's:* Your architect or builder can do these calculations; a lender will more readily believe figures from a person with credentials. Many states and the FHA require such estimates for code compliance or for financing.
   Yearly energy use (Btu = British thermal unit, a standard measure)

   _____

2. *Anticipated yearly energy cost for your home:*

Yearly fuel use		Fuel cost at current prices		Yearly energy cost
$_____	×	$_____	=	$_____

3. *Anticipated yearly energy costs for similar-size conventional house:* your utility can provide this figure. $_____

4. *Anticipated savings for your house:*

Conventional house yearly energy costs (#3)		Earth sheltered yearly energy costs (#2)		Your anticipated yearly savings
$_____	−	$_____	=	$_____

The results of this exercise might again suggest some revision of your design. For example, a particularly costly item like covering the roof with earth may not be reflected in enough energy savings to compensate for the front-end investment (and the financing costs for that investment).

Acquiring a Building Permit

Having selected your contractor, you have all the documents and representatives you need to proceed into the public domain for the necessary approvals, permits, and utility arrangements.

These official processes are triggered by the application for a building permit. You can handle it all or delegate the job to your contractor or to a subcontractor.

The sequence and number of separate stops required to complete the process will vary from one locality to another. You and/or your plans will be routed through various offices to be checked for code compliance and conformance with the zoning ordinances. You will receive an address and legal description of your lot, and you will be scheduled for sewer and water hookup.

Code Compliance

Since application for a permit is in fact made to your local building codes official, it is no surprise that codes are the first set of regulations you will officially confront.

In a large municipality, structural, mechanical, and electrical codes are dealt with by separate individuals. When issued, your permit may only indicate approval of the structural system, in which case your electrical and mechanical contractors must secure their own approvals.

When you call for an appointment with the building codes official, ask how many sets of plans to bring along and what other papers are necessary. A survey of your lot may be required, for example.

If you have done good advance work with the codes official and worked through a design professional, your plans are likely to be approved. Approval may be contingent on certain minor changes that do not require redesign. In this case you simply initial the official's markings. If redesigning is specified, you must decide how to proceed. If you are unable or unwilling to have the changes made, ask how the appeals procedure works. Obtaining a code variance usually involves the state code body and could take a long time.

If you plan to do much of the building yourself or to be your own general contractor, find out from the codes official exactly what inspections will take place and in what sequence. Also ask if there are any restrictions requiring licensed professionals to perform certain parts of the work.

The fee for a building permit will vary according to your locale, and within that locale it may also vary with the size or construction cost of the house. For a $50,000 to $75,000 house in Minneapolis or St. Paul, the fee is in the $400 to $500 range; in Tucson, in the $500 to $600 range.

HUD Minimum Property Standards (MPS) must be met if you intend to seek FHA-insured financing. The building code official will not take care of this aspect. Your plans will not be formally reviewed for compliance by HUD until your lender applies for the FHA loan insurance on your behalf. The architectural section of your HUD area office will informally review your plans earlier, however. To avoid unwelcome surprises, it might be well to take advantage of this service. Your architect or contractor's knowledge of codes and standards could save you such visits unless there are unusual features about which they are unsure.

Zoning Conformance

The issuance of a building permit also depends on compliance with the local zoning ordinances. Frequently the zoning review is handled automatically upon your application for a building permit.

Zoning variances are fairly common, since these ordinances are less critical to life safety than are building codes. Because zoning is locally adopted, enforced, and modified, variances are not too difficult to obtain. You may have to wait, however, for the local governing body or even the affected neighbors to approve a variance. Since the wait can stretch to months if neighbors must be notified and involved, an early inquiry would again be prudent.

Other public business may be transacted during or because of the permit process. If public sewer and water are available where you are building, the arrangements for your service connection will be initiated and you will probably be asked at this point to pay a one-time fee for bringing the connectors to your lot line and initiating service. In Salt Lake City, the fee for sewer availability ranges from $300 to $600, depending on location in the city. In some communities there may be a water availability charge as well; in Salt Lake this fee for an average residence would be about $600.

Your plans may also be subject to design review by a historic preservation commission or community association; permissions for curb cuts may be required. All of these details will be known to your contractor, but you should be aware of the processes and know how much they will cost.

Selection of a good and experienced contractor

7—3. The atrium in the Stow house provides daylighting to the rooms that surround it on all four sides.

(Photo courtesy of John Barnard; reprinted with permission of photographer Phokion Karas, Medford, MA)

can relieve you of some of the above paperwork. Furthermore, both the architect and the contractor can assist you in finding ways to reduce costs if your budget reassessment and energy cost review demonstrate such a necessity. The next step, however, is seeking financing, and here you will be pretty much on your own. Your architect has helped by providing clear and illustrative drawings, and as an extra service, he could accompany you when you present and explain the design to a lender. The responsibility for financing really rests with you, the owner, so the information and suggested strategies in the next chapter should be read and digested with care.

Financing Earth Sheltered Construction

Acquiring financing may be your biggest hurdle before breaking ground. Lenders complain, with apparent justification, of earth sheltered enthusiasts who walk in with plans drawn on a napkin and unsubstantiated stories of huge energy savings. To counter this image, it is imperative that you approach a lender with a knowledgeable and persuasive presentation. In fact, we recommend that you do not approach any lending institution until you clearly understand two things: your own project's strengths, liabilities, and energy-conserving features; and the concerns of the lender.

Following this philosophy, then, the first part of this chapter is background information. Unless you are a banker, you should read through it; home financing is not the same as it used to be.

Today's Changing Financing Picture

Loans

You may need two types of loans when you are building a new home: a construction loan and a mortgage loan. The construction loan, often called *interim financing,* is a short-term loan for up to eighteen months that is usually made at a higher interest rate than a mortgage loan. It is used to draw on for contractor payments during the building. The mortgage loan itself cannot be finally approved until its security, the house, is actually completed according to the plans. The mortgage loan, or *permanent financing,* can be made for a term of up to forty years; it is used to pay off the construction loan.

Construction Loans: Generally your contractor will secure the construction loan but only after your permanent financing is arranged. If you plan to build your own home or act as your own general contractor, you will need to arrange both the construction loan and the permanent mortgage. You should be aware, though, that it is difficult for an owner-builder of even a traditional home to secure construction financing—unless the owner happens to be a professional builder.

The particular lending institution you approach for the two loans may be unwilling to assume the risk for the construction loan but still grant you permanent financing. Should this occur, approach other lenders for the construction loan with your mortgage commitment in hand.

Mortgage Loans: The mortgage lending industry has responded to inflation and fluctuating interest rates by creating a variety of new mortgage instruments that will assure a profit over the life of a mortgage. The traditional fixed-rate, level payment mortgage is still around, but you will also discover a bewildering array of unfamiliar mortgage options called alternative mortgage instruments.

Two generic types of alternative mortgage instruments are identifiable. Mortgages featuring the term *graduated payment* are referred to as GPMs, or more fondly, gyp-ums. The nickname is a bit unfair, since this kind of instrument was designed to allow a first entry into the housing market to people whose income is currently too low but who anticipate increasing incomes. The payments start low and gradually rise at a specified rate over the term of the loan; at their beginning level, they would not be sufficient to fully pay off the loan during the specified term.

When the words *adjustable rate* appear in the title, the loan may involve increasing payment levels but not because the early ones are too low. Rather, the interest rate used to calculate payment amount is allowed to rise (or fall) either on the basis of periodic renegotiation or as a function of periodic adjustment based on the prevailing interest rates.

There are several variations on the above generic mortgage instruments, and entirely new types appear and disappear with some frequency. Moreover, state banking laws vary, and even lenders themselves have some discretion as to how the regulations governing allowable mortgage instruments will be translated into everyday practice.

Given today's fast-changing lending climate, you should take the trouble to inform yourself about new mortgages. Learn what types of loans are being made in your area, how each type works, and what the advantages and disadvantages might be for you. The library is the best source for up-to-date information; check periodicals for articles on real estate and mortgages. Local lending institutions may have pamphlets available describing their programs; realty firms may also be able to assist you.

Institutions

Primary Lenders: The vast majority of single-family mortgage loans are provided by three types of institutions: savings and loan associations and mutual savings banks; commercial banks; and mortgage companies or mortgage bankers. Mortgage companies act as brokers between individual borrowers and remote investors commonly referred to as the *secondary mortgage market*. Rather than hold your mortgage, they package it together with others and immediately sell the package. Savings and loans and commercial banks increasingly need to sell their mortgages as well, so that they can use the proceeds to make more loans. In order to protect the potential marketability of their mortgage loans, then, all such primary lenders will be very careful to meet the secondary investors' standards when making a loan.

Secondary Mortgage Market: For single-family mortgage purchases, the secondary market is mainly comprised of two federally regulated semiprivate institutions: the Federal National Mortgage Association (FNMA, known as Fannie Mae) and the Federal Home Loan Mortgage Corporation (FHLMC, known as Freddie Mac). Private institutions such as insurance companies, and even other lenders also purchase packages of mortgages. All secondary investors' criteria for purchasing home mortgages tend to be determined by the FNMA and FHLMC standards for underwriting and appraisal.

Your lender knows that FHLMC and FNMA are not in business to buy risky loans; their standards are high, and they insist on receiving careful documentation in the appraisal report that supports the primary lender's underwriting decisions. What your lender may not know is that both institutions have purchased energy-conserving home mortgages that meet their standards, including earth sheltered mortgages. Knowing this may improve your lender's receptivity to financing your earth sheltered home.

Lenders' Concerns

Protections against Risk

A lender's primary concern is risk of loss to his own lending institution. The major risk is quite specific: loss in the event that you default on your mortgage. The consequences of borrower default are foreclosure and an immediate need for the lender to sell the property to recoup his remaining investment.

Thus, the broad market appeal of a property is always a critical issue to the lender. An innovative design can present problems because the more your home's appearance departs from the ordinary, or from the appearance of other houses in the neighborhood, the more likely the lender is to question its ready marketability.

To counter this risk, the lender may want the loan to be protected by one of the insurance or guarantee programs operated by the federal government or through the private sector. These programs shift the risk of a loss on a loan default from the private lender to the federal government or private insurer. The loan can be granted with a lower down payment than if the risk were all on the private lender.

Federal Insurance or Guarantee Programs: The Federal Housing Administration (FHA) does not make loans; it insures the lender's loan. *FHA has insured loans on earth sheltered homes.* The Veterans Administration (VA) will guarantee a lender against loss for up to 60 percent of the loan. VA loans have no minimum down payment requirement. *VA has guaranteed loans on earth sheltered homes.* As in the FHA program, the home must meet HUD's Minimum Property Standards.

Private Mortgage Insurance: If you plan to apply for a conventional loan (one made without recourse to FHA or VA), your lender's risk can also be protected through private mortgage insurance.

Private mortgage insurers generally insure only the top 20 to 25 percent of a mortgage. This is usually sufficient for the lender to recoup his money even after sale of the property at a reduced price. *Earth sheltered loans have been privately insured already:* your lender should be told this.

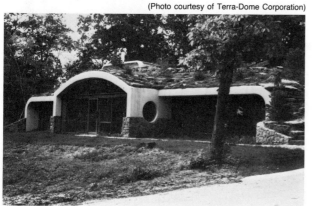

8—1. Terra-Dome Corporation offers homes like this four-bedroom model through a dealer network and its own traveling work crews. The 24- by 24-foot modules that make up their standard designs can be rearranged as desired.

(Photo courtesy of Terra-Dome Corporation)

(Photo courtesy of Terra-Dome Corporation)

8—2. Terra-Dome modules can also be adapted for multifamily configurations, like the triplex whose entry is shown above. Very little of this building is visible from the single-family Terra-Dome model in the background, although the triplex is right in its front yard.

Express your willingness to incur the cost for either federal or private mortgage insurance. Your lending institution will apply for the insurance on your behalf. The alternative to loan insurance or guarantees is a higher down payment. This also reduces the lender's exposure should a foreclosed property have to be sold.

Professional Certification: A second risk of loss confronts the lender, again quite a specific one. Even if your payments are not in default, he may still inherit the house if you later have structural or waterproofing failures so serious that you walk away from it. If you intend to build the house yourself, he will have second thoughts about both the sturdiness and the timeliness of completion. If the design is also your own work, you will surely be facing an uphill fight.

Your lender's best protection against structural failure is the same as your own: the experience and qualifications of competent professionals in both design and construction. If the design is your own, reassure him by having your plans reviewed and certified by a qualified engineer or architect before you present them.

Criteria for Evaluating your Project

The overriding criterion used by the lender to judge your proposed property is its market value. The loan officer will have a professional appraiser estimate the market value and then will use this figure in setting the amount and terms of the loan. The importance of the market value makes the appraiser, with whom you are unlikely to deal directly, one of the most important professionals involved in the success of your project.

The market value indicated by the appraiser's estimate is the amount the lender could recoup if you defaulted. If your project cost is higher than the appraised (market) value, then a loan amount to cover such a cost would be partially at risk if default occurs. In the event the appraisal is lower than your agreed-on cost, the lender may ask you to make up the difference (and thus eliminate his exposure) with a higher down payment.

Market value is an estimate of what a buyer will pay. It is not the same thing as the cost of construction or the selling price.

Several factors work to lower appraised value on an innovative structure. To make his estimate, the appraiser's preferred approach is to compare your project with similar, recently sold properties in the area, called *comparables*. By adjusting the selling price of each comparable to allow for its differences with your property, he arrives at your project's estimated value. In the absence of good comparables (i.e., earth sheltered ones), he may have to use another approach, but being unable to observe demonstrated values, he may well be conservative in his resulting estimate.

Like all residential properties, your home (or more accurately, your lot and your house plans) will be judged for neighborhood compatibility, design appeal, and overall livability. Does your proposed

8–3. Floor plan of the triplex, showing the covered atrium shared by two of the units. More information about Terra-Dome is in Appendix C.

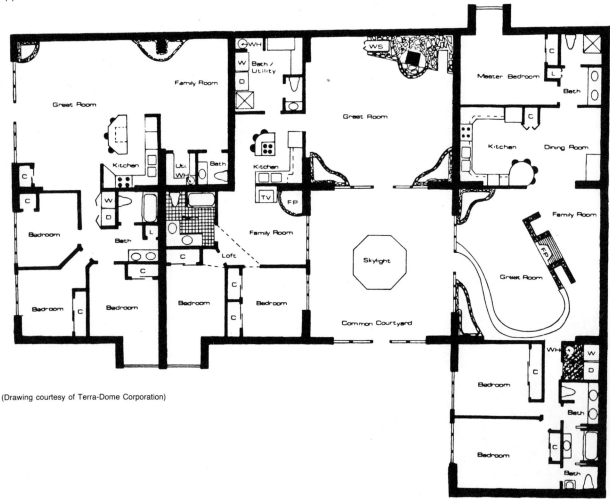

(Drawing courtesy of Terra-Dome Corporation)

home fit prevailing tastes, the specific site, the neighborhood? Have you included enough daylighting and proper ventilation to counter the "cave image"? An appraiser may lower the value of an earth sheltered home if he believes its unusual design will reduce its appeal to the average buyer.

Last, the extent to which the added cost of energy-conserving features will be recognized in the market may be at issue. Future buyers might not be willing to make an equivalent investment in energy features that are not visible because they are integral to the structure itself. For example, will the average buyer understand that the dark quarry tile on the floor in front of a south window is a solar collector and not just decorating finish? Such features could fall into the class of items appraisers call overimprovements. Tennis courts and swimming pools are also overimprovements.

There is far more history for estimating market value versus original cost for tennis courts, however, than there is for innovative energy investments. Therefore, if you anticipate significant energy savings, be prepared to document the dollar value of the savings from your home's energy-conserving features and your resulting ability to shift utility dollars to increased monthly mortgage payments.

Remember, lenders usually do not allow you to commit over 28 percent of income to your basic housing expense. FHLMC underwriting guidelines suggest, however, that for energy-efficient properties the borrower may make payments that exceed 28 percent provided the energy efficiency is well documented in the appraisal report. Use this point in negotiating the terms of your mortgage.

A higher percentage of income means higher monthly payments; in this case you would be financing your additional investment in energy-conserving features through a larger mortgage. Alternatively, the ability to make higher monthly payments might allow you to keep the mortgage amount constant but reduce your down payment.

Shopping for a Lending Institution

The first rule in looking for a lender is: if you have a long-standing relationship with a particular institution, go there first. Someone who knows your financial track record may be more receptive to an innovative project.

The second rule: do the preliminary work early, and be prepared to shop. Compare terms, costs, and the reception you receive.

The third rule: do your homework before your first contact. As suggested before, update yourself on the new mortgage instruments so that you can ask questions about the particular type of loan you think you want. Also have at your fingertips the financial information you calculated in chapter 5 and the project costs as assessed in chapter 7.

To locate institutions that may be open-minded about your project, ask your architect or contractor; pay attention to individual institutions' advertising; and check with other energy-conserving home buyers, your energy agency, or your utility company to see if any lending institutions are cooperating with them in providing mortgages or home improvement loans in connection with energy-conservation programs.

Identify the institutions you want to approach and the type of mortgage for which you wish to apply as soon in your process as you can, preferably after you have accepted the design and have the architect's cost estimate. Then start canvassing the institutions, as described below.

Making Your Presentation

Make an appointment with the loan officer at the likeliest institution. When you call for your appointment, be prepared to answer readily any possible questions, including the type and location of the house, the construction and total project budget, the type of loan you wish to apply for, and how much down payment and monthly housing expense you can afford. Ask what documents to bring along and how many copies you will need.

Presenting Information on Your Personal Finances

Necessary Financial Information: As with any home mortgage loan, your personal financial position and thus your ability to repay the loan is absolutely critical. If you are known to be solidly creditworthy, the loan officer may not be overly concerned about the unusual aspects of your design.

With regard to your credit, the loan officer wants to know three basic things: if you can afford the monthly payments, if you have ready cash to handle the transaction costs, and if you meet your obligations. To fill out the residential loan application, information about your individual or family financial history and current and potential employment situation will be necessary. Expanding on the personal

Surveying Lenders

Call each lending institution, ask for a loan officer (a loan originator at a mortgage company), record his or her name and number in case you will be calling back, and then ask these questions:

- What type of home mortgage loans are you offering?
- What is the lowest down payment required to secure a loan?
- What is your interest rate today?

You will find that types of mortgages and terms vary widely, and the information you receive may be complex. Use the worksheet to record the answers you receive.

The loan officer may ask you a number of questions in return. Answer as best you can (you may not have completely accurate responses as yet), and indicate you will have better information when you are ready to call for an actual appointment.

	A	B	C	D
Lending institution				
Contact/Phone number				
Type of loan				
Terms/Down payment				
Interest rate				

financial assessment you completed in chapter 5, do the following activity in preparation for completing that form.

Financial Items to Bring: Most of the information you will need to bring is listed below. Add any other items requested, and assemble the materials into packets that can be left behind.

- Cash or personal check for credit investigation and appraisal fee (ask the loan officer for the specific amounts; each will be $100 to $150)

- Information on your last two years' residence, including address and phone number of landlord, if applicable
- Information on your last two years' income and employment, including:
  current and past gross salary figures
  employers' names, addresses, and
      phone number
  the above for coapplicant or spouse
  any other source of income
- Information on the value of all assets, including:
  life insurance policies
  investments (you may be asked to bring
      the certificates)
  income property or business inventory
      and equipment
  personal property such as cars, boats,
      household furnishings, etc.
  bank accounts (bring account numbers,
      name and address of depositories)
  pensions and burial funds
- Information on all debts, including name and address of firm, account numbers, unpaid balances, monthly payments

Presenting Information on Your Project

If you are concerned that the energy-conserving items or the uniqueness of your design may raise questions, consider the strategies below.

Educate Your Lender and Appraiser: Prepare a small information packet on earth sheltering for loan officers who are unfamiliar with this building technique. The goal is to lend credibility to your project by showing the lender that it is not an anomaly or a fad.

The packet could include a copy of one of the many available books on earth sheltering. Bring information on the number, location, and actual energy performance of earth sheltered homes in the region, and perhaps even photographs.

A description of your project's energy strategy would be helpful. An appraiser often appraises three to four homes a day; any information you can provide that will help him quickly understand the unique features of your property will be useful. To explain your energy investment, write a brief description of the design's energy-related features and their purpose. Attach the worksheet you prepared when assessing your energy costs and savings (in chapter 7), and ask the loan officer to provide this information to the appraiser.

Confront Potential Appraisal Problems: If you anticipate that the appraiser may be unfamiliar with earth sheltering and with techniques for estimating market values of innovative projects, there are several steps you can take.

1. Locate and submit addresses of several earth sheltered comparables to help the appraiser begin. Ideal comparables will appeal to the same market segment; have an equally desirable location; be similar in size, design, and energy-conserving features; and will have sold within the last year.
2. Consider submitting an independent appraisal from a certified appraiser experienced with properties similar to yours. This will be an added cost, and there is no guarantee that the lender's appraiser will concur, but it may serve as a useful basis for comparison.
3. If the loan is rejected or the terms are unfavorable because of an appraisal that you think undervalues the property, request a second appraisal. Some institutions will not allow this practice; others will accommodate you but will also charge for the second appraisal. You will probably have to accept the result of the second appraisal as final, whether it is higher or lower than the first.

Property Items to Bring: Before your meet with a loan officer, ask what kinds of property items to bring and how many copies of each. The packet of materials you prepare will include the items listed below (the last four being optional).

- Information about the lot, including property description, purchase agreement if applicable, proof of ownership, title insurance policy, if applicable
- Copies of house plans and specifications (the number required will vary; VA and FHA require three)
- Engineer or architect's certification of plans, if needed
- Copy of construction contract and builder's phone number
- Contractor's certified cost estimates (sworn construction statement)
- Energy description plus cost and savings worksheet
- Brief information packet on earth sheltering
- Your own list of comparables
- Property appraisal by a certified appraiser

Financial Assessment

Describe your credit history and be honest. Serious credit problems or chronically late mortgage payments will be uncovered by the lending institution. It is better to bring up the problems and how they were overcome yourself. List significant credit factors, positive and negative.

Positive	Negative

Describe your employment history and assess your future potential. Have you had frequent job changes that will need to be discussed? Can you anticipate an increasing income? Outline your history and potential here.

History	Potential

Finally, do not forget that the decision of a mortgage lender to commit funds to any house is a determination of risk. Although your project may be innovative, if it is also well thought out, you should be able to obtain a mortgage. Do not be discouraged by one lender's rejection. Learn from it, adjust your house plans if necessary, and then continue to shop around for the lending institution that will offer you acceptable terms.

Chapter 9

The Construction Process

With an approved design, a contractor hired, and your financing arranged, you are finally ready to break ground. If your research, planning, learning, designing, assessing, and negotiating up to this point have been patient and thorough, you will already have anticipated and solved many potential construction problems.

Even though competent, trusted professionals are building the house and monitoring its progress, you should not relax yet. Any earth sheltered building project contains enormous opportunities for errors in the field, both small and large. There is no substitute for the owner's frequent presence and wary eye at the job site.

The Owner's Role during Construction

Many contractors understandably prefer working for themselves by building homes "on speculation" rather than for a specific owner. What they thereby avoid are continual owner site inspections, change orders, and a potential withholding of the last portion of the fee (usually also the contractor's profit) until the owner is satisfied.

All of these potentially adversarial conditions are going to be present on your job site. The obvious strategies for avoiding such difficulties are, of course, to have selected your contractor partly for compatibility in the first place; and to use common sense, patience, and courtesy to nurture a sense of partnership in an intriguing venture. Beyond these, what is the appropriate role for the earth sheltered home owner during the construction process?

Decision Making

Your contractual agreement spells out the architect/owner/contractor relationship and probably assigns the owner a voice in any change of plans or correction of errors. Use it. Be available for making decisions and let your views be known.

To avoid headaches, both your own and the contractor's, stick to the plans and specifications as closely as possible. Major changes can be extremely costly and minor ones a nuisance, especially when materials have already been ordered.

Monitoring Progress

In addition to being the final decision maker when problems arise, the owner should also function as

111

a kind of early warning system, checking the site frequently for signs of potential problems.

The architect cannot be on-site for every single construction step. On the other hand, the eye of an untrained observer may be unable to distinguish a possible construction mistake from a normal condition. Since the owner is likely to visit the site much more frequently, however, a good system can be developed that features an owner scouting anything that looks suspicious and calling the architect to check.

Under no circumstances should the owner supervise the work, unless this is specifically provided for in the contract. Monitoring potential problems and checking with the architect are very different from supervising or directing the crew. Supervision is strictly the responsibility and privilege of the contractor.

Paying the Contractor

The payment schedule as specified in the contract relies on the owner and architect's satisfaction with work completed to date. You have the right to withhold payment until work is satisfactorily completed according to the plans.

You also have an obligation to be prompt in meeting the payment schedule or else to be very specific as to what problems must be corrected before payment will be made. If the contractor cannot pay subcontractors promptly, or for his own reasons does not do so, the unpaid subcontractors have the right to place a lien on your property. A lien placed by an unpaid subcontractor is called a mechanic's lien. It is filed in the Registrar of Deed's office. Some states require that you be notified when a lien is filed; others do not. The lien is placed on the real estate (both land and house) rather than on your personal property. If he wishes to, an unpaid subcontractor who has filed a mechanic's lien can go to court and, in effect, institute a foreclosure, forcing the sale of the house to pay off the obligation, whether it be $500 or $10,000. An existing lien may not be acted upon immediately but will be discovered if and when you sell the property. Your seller may be scared off, or you might arrange that the obligation be paid off by deducting it from the purchase price.

To avoid entangling yourself in these difficulties, there is a simple precaution you can take. As payments are made to the contractor, you should ask for and receive copies of subcontractors' lien waivers (or partial lien waivers) indicating they have been fully or partially paid. Upon final payment ask for copies of all the subcontractors' final lien waivers, indicating that you (and your financial institution) now own the building without encumbrance.

Observing Construction

Who Observes

Your architect is the best observer of construction; this service is normally included in his fee. The $600 to $1,000 that normally comprises the observation portion of the fee could, in fact, be the most cost-effective part of his service. Most errors occur in the field; the cost for observation could very quickly be exceeded by the cost in dollars, time, headaches, and potential future consequences of unnoticed and uncorrected mistakes.

There is a lingering perception that an architect not only observes but supervises construction for an owner. Though common in the past, architect supervision is no longer practiced today. The American Institute of Architects, in an effort to clarify liability, has redefined the architect's role to be that of an observer, leaving supervision to the contractor.

The professional's eye is important on any residential building project, but the likely inexperience of the crews with some earth sheltering procedures makes professional observation even more important. There is ample room for misinterpretation of the drawings, especially when it comes to unfamiliar details such as the correct application of waterpoofing or flashing around the penetrations on an earth-covered roof.

The architect's observation is often supplemented by that of his consulting or staff engineer for the parts of the design in the engineer's jurisdiction. For example, the size, placement, and tying of reinforcing steel rods within the concrete and the pouring of the concrete itself will involve the design engineer. Some lenders who finance earth sheltered mortgages require such observation.

Official observations in the form of inspections will occur periodically throughout construction. The building code inspector's visits should be timed by the contractor to occur just before the item to be inspected vanishes behind a wall. There will likely be inspection after excavation and footings are done, of rough electrical and plumbing lines, of the structural system, and subsequent spot checks of finished work. A final inspection when the building is substantially complete is necessary for the issuance of an occupancy permit.

In addition, the appraiser may visit during construction and must make a final inspection before pronouncing the home satisfactorily completed. If you are financing your home through VA or FHA, their inspectors will visit to determine that the project as built meets their standards.

In many ways you are the most importnat member of the observation team. You will visit your site as often as possible anyway, preferably with your camera and notebook as well as a set of plans and specifications. Your purpose is not to pester the contractor and his crew, but showing up unannounced at varying times of the day and evening will effectively remind them of your concern.

What to Watch for

If you are like most earth sheltered home owners, you probably have taken the time to learn and understand as much as possible about building techniques and energy systems. Initially, as the descriptions at the end of this chapter illustrate, the variety of structural materials, waterproofing, and insulating products boggle the mind. By this stage, however, you and your professional advisors have made choices. When you arrive at the construction site, you need understand only the materials and techniques you have chosen for your own home.

The plans and specifications are your best guide, assuming you have insisted that they be as complete and detailed as possible. Although you may never have to become proficient at reading working drawings in general, you can learn to use your own as a reference point.

What to watch for when you have little experience to guide you, then, is how closely the contractor has adhered to the drawings and specifications. The following examples of embarrassing mistakes illustrate a further point: common sense and an objective eye will detect possible errors that the contractor may simply be too closely involved to see.

A mistake concerning the size of footings occurred when a contractor misread the specification that footings be "a minimum depth of four feet." He used massive amounts of unnecessary concrete for footings four feet high, rather than simply placing them at a four-foot depth below the surface.

Errors in the construction of poured concrete walls are occasionally reported: in most cases the problems result from incorrect or careless placement of reinforcing steel. An inadequately reinforced wall is likely to collapse, especially during backfilling (the replacement of earth around the outside).

Common sense should also dictate that while the backfilling is going on, the walls will be under extra stress. Temporary bracing from the inside has sometimes been neglected or forgotten, often with the result that walls deflect inward and either collapse or throw the building out of square. Even bracing may not prevent uneven stresses from bending walls if backfill is placed and compacted in uneven segments around the building; neglecting to compact soil in successive layers can lead to uneven settlement later. Rough dumping of the backfill material can damage the waterproofing or insulation on the outside of the structure.

The catalog of errors is potentially limitless, and an owner's best insurance is of course to have hired an experienced contractor who has already made his mistakes—on someone else's project. For the rest, constant observation and a willingness to keep asking questions of the appropriate party are the keys to avoiding expensive mistakes.

A word about guarantees: they are reassuring, and if they are supported by testing and the products they back are repairable by normally skilled technicians, then you could be more swayed by guarantees in your choice of materials. Even a ten-year guarantee is meaningless, however, if the company providing it has gone out of business. Furthermore, frequently only the product itself is replaced; the cost of digging back in to find a failed waterproofing product and any associated damage to the structure, for example, may not be covered.

Never be bought or sold by a guarantee. Make sure the guarantors are reliable and stable, and depend on having the product installed or applied correctly the first time.

The construction processes that need monitoring by a professional should be agreed on with the architect before building starts. For example, your architect or engineer should certainly be on hand during poured wall construction to check the placement and tying of steel reinforcing, the roughing in of ducts, electrical conduit and plumbing connections, and the mix characteristics of the concrete to be poured.

The waterproofing process should be observed by the architect, as mistakes here are also common. Waterproofing membranes that must adhere directly to a roof surface have been found laid over piles of sweepings; seams have been inadequately sealed. Since potential waterproofing problems are usually covered quickly in the normal process of construction, it could be months before they are discovered.

Construction Materials and Procedures

In chapter 2 we offered a cursory description of the anatomy of an earth sheltered house, highlighting building materials and processes that may differ from those used in conventional construction. Knowing more about these materials and procedures is helpful in assessing the implications of your schematic design and particularly important for adequate construction observation.

The further descriptions in this section will provide you with a working vocabulary for communicating with professionals you encounter during your entire process, especially the codes official, the architect, and the contractor. Here is an interesting feedback loop. Learning what construction (the end of the process) involves helps you understand the implications of site and design choices at the beginning.

Structural Materials

The most commonly used structural material for earth sheltering is concrete. It is durable, strong, fire-resistant, and provides valuable mass for thermal storage.

Cast-in-Place: Concrete that is poured, or cast, at the site offers flexibility of building shape. The construction of the forms to hold the concrete while it sets is an expensive part of the poured concrete system, however. Traditional poured wall contractors have standard, reusable forms to reduce such costs. At least one earth sheltered builder, Terra-Dome Corporation, has a patented reusable forming system that offers similar economy for the poured walls and dome-shaped roofs incorporated into their designs.

Without the reinforcement supplied by steel bars placed inside the forms before pouring, plain cast-in-place systems are appropriate only for floors on grade, walls with little earth cover, and normal-size footings. With proper reinforcing, however, walls at any depth can be cast in place; with reinforcing, horizontal structural elements like larger footings, intermediate floors, and even roofs can also be poured at the site.

Advantages of cast-in-place concrete are:

- it is available nearby in most areas
- structural components, if all cast in place, can be tightly tied together

- potential waterproofing problems are reduced since surfaces are smooth and unjointed

The disadvantages of cast-in-place systems include the possibilities that:

- cracks from shrinkage or shifting could occur
- curing time could delay construction
- higher interior humidity will occur in the first months as the concrete fully dries out
- cold-weather work could be difficult

Post-Tensioned Concrete: This is a variation on the cast-in-place system. The difference is that in post tensioning, cast-in-place concrete is placed in constant tension by means of tightening the rein-

(Photo courtesy of Terra-Dome Corporation)

9—1. Terra-Dome Corporation's form system for one of the 24-by 24-foot modules used in its house plans.

9—2. Poured concrete is reinforced by the placement of steel reinforcing bars inside the forms prior to pouring the concrete. Footings, such as those shown formed and reinforced here, are examples of horizontal structural elements whose capabilities for support are increased by proper reinforcing.

forcing rods after the concrete is poured. The advantages are the same as for cast-in-place systems, with the further benefit that the potential for cracking is reduced and the structural elements are tied together very tightly. A disadvantage over cast-in-place systems is that the cost may be slightly higher. Simmons and Sun, Inc., a construction and consulting firm in Missouri, uses this system in the earth sheltered homes they build (see Appendix C).

Precast Concrete: Precast materials are formed and cured at the plant, transported to the site, and then assembled there. Their use allows quick and possibly less expensive construction if your site is near the plant and accessible to cranes.

Precast materials come in a variety of forms, the most commonly used being prestressed planks. A 40-inch-wide plank with hollow cores is in fact the most common earth-covered roof material of all:

the longitudinal cores not only lighten the plank but also can double as utility distribution spaces. Often roof planks are covered with a thin poured concrete topping that adds strength, smooths the surface for waterproofing, and slopes slightly for good drainage. Both hollow-core and solid planks are used for walls as well.

Advantages of precast concrete over cast-in-place systems include:

- shorter construction time
- economy and normally good quality control because of mass production
- the elimination of curing delay
- the possibility of cold-weather assembly

Disadvantages are:

- the joints between the components require careful attention
- planks and panels are bulky to ship and to manipulate at the site
- their usually flat form limits design flexibility

Masonry: The term masonry describes the work, in stones, bricks, or blocks, of a mason. In this context masonry refers to concrete blocks. Without reinforcing, concrete block is suitable only for walls with little earth cover and for non-load-bearing interior partitions. With reinforcing, however, block walls are fairly common for one-story structures and can be used in properly designed two-story structures.

9—3. Prestressed hollow-core planks being hoisted into place for a roof.

9—4. Steel-reinforced or prestressed concrete panels are also available. This one has insulation sandwiched inside. Panels are used for walls and sometimes even for roofs.

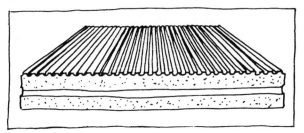

9—5. Dry-stacked concrete blocks. In theory the strong exterior mortar has the effect of reinforcing the dry-stacked wall, although some failures have been reported.

(Photo courtesy of Don Metz)

9—6. An interior view of the Earthtech house shown in figures 2–12 and 2–13, designed by Don Metz, a Lyme, NH, architect. Massive wood beams support the roof. Detailed plans are available; see Appendix C.

Conventionally mortared block walls are most commonly used, but it is also possible to dry-stack the blocks; that is, to lay the blocks without any mortar between them and then to apply a strong fiberglass-reinforced mortar to both the inside and outside surfaces of the wall. The advantages of concrete block are:

- it is available fairly readily and cheaply since it is mass produced
- it can be assembled into complex shapes
- it is fairly strong

Its disadvantages are:

- a block wall requires very good waterproofing

- curing time for the mortar may delay construction
- laying block in cold weather is more difficult

Wood: For interior structural support in the form of columns or beams, the warmth, color, and strength of wood make it a pleasing choice. It provides less mass for thermal storage than concrete does but is a good complement to tile, masonry, or poured concrete floors, walls, and ceilings.

Pressure-treated wood is sometimes used instead of concrete as a structural material for the exterior shell. Everstrong Marketing, Inc., a Minnesota earth sheltered building company, makes a good case for all-wood construction. More information can be procured by contacting the company.

(Photo courtesy of Everstrong Marketing, Inc.)

9–7. An earth sheltered house in Redwood Falls, MN, by Everstrong Marketing, Inc. is constructed of pressure-treated wood. Currently used as the company office, the 1,040–square foot structure costs approximately $75 per year to heat.

Advantages of wood for structural systems are:

● it is familiar to contractors
● its light weight allows smaller footings
● it can be handled in cold weather
● it can be less costly than concrete

Disadvantages are:

● it requires chemical treatment
● it is combustible
● it requires extensive nailing and gluing for adequate strength
● it provides little mass for thermal storage

Waterproofing

The Underground Space Center at the University of Minnesota has produced two *Fact Sheets* devoted to waterproofing. The *Fact Sheets* are part of a series of twelve on earth sheltering done for the U.S. Department of Energy by the Underground Space Center and by the Center for Natural Energy Design at Oklahoma State University. The two booklets on waterproofing outline considerations, materials, and techniques in valuable detail.

Even with the amount of information contained in these highly recommended booklets, however, the Underground Space Center suggests that the layperson's best protection against leaks is to take advantage of the skills, experience, and intuition of a professional. Waterproofing, cautions the Center, "is an art as much as a science." Choosing the right approach depends not only on the particulars of your own climate, site, soil conditions, and design, but also on correct selection from a mind-boggling array of products, only some of which function well below grade.

The following discussion is not intended to be a primer on how to waterproof; whole books can be written on the subject. In fact, the liveliest of arguments, even among experts at earth sheltering conferences, center around the complexities of product selection and use.

The purpose of this section is rather to underscore the opinions that the experts do share about waterproofing: that choosing the correct product or products for the watertight membrane itself is only part of the battle. Just as important is the drainage plan, the design and preparation of the exterior surface, and the protection provided after the waterproof skin has been applied. Although the complexities certainly suggest that your waterproofing plan is best done by a professional, it is also apparent that there are a number of concerns you can profitably bring to the assessment of your design as well as the monitoring of your construction progress.

Landscape Design and Drainage: Preventing water from even approaching the building's exterior surface is the first and best defense against leaks. Contouring the land surface to route water away from your house is one such preventive measure. A dip or depression, called a *swale*, can be created on the earth's surface behind the back wall (see fig. 9-8). The drainage swale allows surface runoff either to be diverted around the house and down the slope or else held and drained away before reaching the exterior walls.

Providing a zone of quickly draining soil around

9–8. The first line of defense against leaks starts not at the building wall but rather in the soil surrounding the house.

(From *Earth Sheltered Structures Fact Sheets*, #3, "Waterproofing Techniques.")

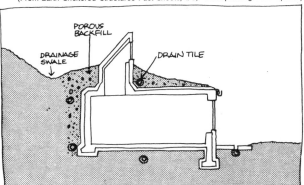

the building is another important strategy in most areas. This is cheapest when the soil excavated from the site itself is permeable and can be used as the backfill material. The porous backfill is compacted in layers to prevent settlement or slumping that could displace the actual waterproofing material; often the capping layer will consist of a less permeable kind of soil.

When water does reach the building walls or roof, it must be drained away promptly. Water that collects and remains in the soil above a flat roof surface, for example, could eventually find a way in. A 1-inch rainfall can deposit 5 pounds per square foot of water on an earth-covered roof. A porous backfill spread just above the final waterproofing layers is important for quick horizontal drainage. A slightly sloped roof surface provides additional assistance in draining water off. Drain tiles running horizontally through the soil around the walls provide outlets for water draining off the roof and otherwise into and through the backfill.

Structure: Curved exterior surfaces will limit your product choices for waterproofing and insulation. Moreover, the various structural materials each involve some limitations since they cure, flex, and settle differently. You and your designer therefore need to consider the implications for waterproofing of your design choices regarding the form of the building.

No matter what the design choices, further insurance against leaks will include limiting the number of roof penetrations and taking care to provide drainage whenever "dams" are created by such structural features as skylights, retaining walls, and parapet walls at the front edge of roofs. Critical points such as penetrations, transitions from one structural surface to another, or joints between structural elements like precast plank are probably the most frequent sources of leaks. The design of the waterproofing details at these points must be attended to carefully.

Finally, the surface on which the watertight material will be applied must be carefully prepared. In your drawings, for example, the concrete's surface looks smooth. On the job site, though, it is probably somewhat bumpy, notched, and greasy. Since the waterproofing materials chosen should bond or adhere directly, the surface may need to be smoothed, patched, and cleaned. Adhesion to the entire surface is an important characteristic to look for in choosing a product for the waterproof membrane. Should water somehow leak through it, you want to avoid

the possibility that the water will travel behind the membrane and appear somewhere else inside the structure. Being able to locate the exact source of a leak is important when repair will also require excavation.

Waterproofing Membrane: There is no single best material for waterproofing. Each one has advantages and disadvantages to be weighed in the context of your soil, your structure's shape and materials, the experience of the installation crew, and the weather conditions expected during its application. Remember to evaluate its cost, projected life span, and availability as well.

Ordinary plastic sheeting, dampproofing coatings, and built-up asphalt or pitch are not effective for below-grade use by themselves. Materials that are appropriate under certain conditions include such generic products as cementitious materials, liquid elastomers, modified bitumens, vulcanates, and bentonite clay products. Within each category are often a number of specific types of products, each in turn appearing on the market under several different brand names.

Cementitious materials are cement compounds that are sprayed or troweled onto the surface of concrete or masonry, penetrating slightly and forming a fine crystalline structure within the voids of the concrete.

Advantages: cementitious materials

- have moderate material cost
- have low to moderate labor cost
- require only common labor
- have long life span
- can be repaired from inside the structure

Disadvantages:

- have limited ability to bridge cracks or reseal
- have very little flexibility
- do not provide vapor barrier
- can be used only on concrete and masonry surfaces

Liquid elastomers, including urethanes, elastomerics, rubbers, and resins, are applied in liquid form and cure to a flexible, monolithic membrane.

Advantages: liquid elastomers

- have moderate labor cost

- are easily applied to curved or complex surfaces
- bond well to properly prepared surfaces
- have good life spans for highest quality products
- resist most chemical and physical damage

Disadvantages:

- highest quality are moderate to high in cost
- do not reseal or span large cracks
- give off toxic fumes during application and curing
- are sensitive to temperature, humidity, and precipitation during curing
- require fully cured and finely finished surfaces
- may require two coats
- acrylic latex-based elastomers may break down from prolonged exposure
- poor quality control of many products and applicators

Modified bitumens, also known as rubberized asphalt, usually come in rolls, and may be laminated to one or more polyethylene backing sheets. The material is fully bonded to the structure, and overlapped seams are also bonded.

Advantages: modified bitumens

- have moderate material and labor cost
- have uniform thickness and consistency
- bridge cracks well
- resist most soil conditions
- may be applied to concrete, masonry, metals, and wood
- have long life span if properly applied

Disadvantages:

- require smooth, clean, and dry surface
- should not be applied under cold or damp conditions
- should be applied to slightly sloped surfaces to drain since seams are formed by overlapping
- must be covered quickly to protect polyethylene from ultraviolet degradation
- are combustible

Vulcanates include a variety of fully cured or "vulcanized" elastomers, polymers, and rubber compounds. Vulcanate membranes (compounds such as Butyl, EPDM, neoprene and Hypalon) have specific individual characteristics, but in general come either in roll stock or in sheets that are seamed at

the site, or as a single factory-seamed membrane that is unfolded.

Advantages: vulcanates

- enable high quality control and consistency
- are tough, flexible, and have good crack-bridging characteristics
- resist most chemicals, environmental degradation, soil fungi, and bacteria
- have a broad range of application temperatures
- may be used for flashings
- have high impermeability (except neoprene)
- work well on dead level surfaces

Disadvantages:

- have high material and labor costs
- are hard to apply over projections, penetrations, complex forms
- allow water to travel behind the membrane, making it difficult to locate leaks, should they occur
- are difficult to seam adequately in the field
- require proper weather for application and assembly
- may be sensitive to solvents and sun exposure
- require clean, dry, smooth surfaces for application when adhered
- need special accessories for penetrations and flashings

Bentonite clay products are made from a base of dry, granular bentonite clay. Bentonite swells when wet, forming a highly impermeable, dense, pastelike material. It returns to its original volume when dry. It may be sprayed or troweled onto the building. A panel application, featuring the confinement of raw bentonite within a corrugated cardboard panel that is intended to decay and leave the clay in place, is probably best used only under slabs or on vertical surfaces, where a rush of water will not wash the clay away after the panel decays.

Advantages: bentonite clay products

- have moderate material and labor costs
- have excellent resealing and crack bridging properties
- adhere well to surfaces
- have no application temperature restrictions
- have a short curing time

- do not allow leaks to travel
- can be applied by unskilled labor (troweled on only)
- conform to complex forms (except panels)
- have no seams or joints (except panels)
- can be applied horizontally or vertically
- may be repaired from inside the structure
- can be used on any surface

Disadvantages:

- cannot be used in high salinity soils
- should not be used in hot, arid climates subject to sudden downpours
- must be protected from extensive wetting prior to backfill
- cannot be applied on wet foundations or where water is running
- have high equipment cost for spray application
- must be immediately backfilled or covered with polyethylene film or spray mastic
- cannot be exposed above grade and so must be covered with flashing
- reduce future options for waterproofing repair or replacement because removal is messy and difficult

Given the differing characteristics of the various waterproofing products, many designs will specify certain materials for roofs, different ones for walls, and special treatments for critical areas such as the transition on a wall between above- and below-grade areas or around penetrations.

Protection of the Waterproofing: According to the experts at the Underground Space Center, the waterproof skin for an earth sheltered house preferably consists of a sequence of materials similar to the Protected Membrane Roof system frequently used

9—9. Once the proper combination of waterproofing materials has been applied, a common approach is to apply insulation over them for protection. This section of an exterior wall shows schematic waterproofing membrane and insulation.

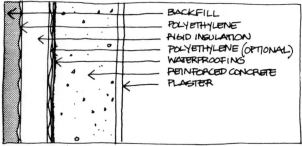

BACKFILL
POLYETHYLENE
RIGID INSULATION
POLYETHYLENE (OPTIONAL)
WATERPROOFING
REINFORCED CONCRETE
PLASTER

(From *Earth Sheltered Structures Fact Sheets*, #4, "Waterproofing Considerations and Materials.")

on above-grade flat roofs. The watertight membrane, no matter what it is made of, should be shielded from potentially adverse below-grade conditions.

Protecting the membrane often involves at least two layers: plastic sheeting for an extra moisture barrier and for help in containing the watertight material, and a layer of rigid insulation. Insulation board insulates the membrane from potentially damaging freeze-thaw cycles, it prevents damage to the sometimes fragile material during backfilling or from tree roots, and it may deflect some incidental water problems. Often sheets of polyethylene are overlapped as further protection over the insulation layer.

Insulation

The choice of insulating material that may be in direct contact with earth is limited by the fact that wetness severely reduces the heat resistance value (R value) of many products. Rigid panels of extruded polystyrene (Styrofoam and Thermax are familiar brand names) absorb the least moisture. This material is more expensive than beadboard (expanded polystyrene), for example, but it performs better over a longer period of time.

The appropriate amount of insulation varies according to climate and ground temperature. In warm climates, where heat loss through the walls, floor, and roof is often desired, little or no insulation would be used; in the coldest climates, up to R-40 insulation could be considered for the parts of the building with the least soil cover. Insulation need not be applied with uniform thickness over the entire structure. The idea is to equalize the amount of heat loss through each part of the envelope, so more deeply buried surfaces need lesser amounts.

Mentioning every conceivable consideration and caution about construction materials and procedures is not possible here. Indeed, it is not even desirable; a little knowledge, especially in the area of waterproofing, can be hazardous. The idea is to gain enough understanding to discuss and probe but to rely on your professionals for detailed knowledge and experience (if you are interested in learning more, see Appendix A).

Since the entire process of construction varies too much from house to house to describe in any but rather useless general terms, we have chosen to illustrate the process by means of a particular example. The next chapter is where you will be able, finally, to see what happened first, what happened next, and so on until a particular house was completed.

Chapter 10

A Sample Construction Project

In general, the process of building an underground house is like setting a fence post. You dig a hole wider than the post, place the post in the hole, and fill the soil firmly back in around it. Similarly, an earth sheltered house is built by excavating an area larger than the house, building the whole house in the excavation, and filling the earth back around and over it.

Preconstruction Preparation

Having emphasized the complexity of the earth sheltered building sequence throughout this book, we now need a little perspective. The building of a conventional wood-frame house is just as complex, but builders have been using essentially the same techniques for many years and know from experience how to organize the work for efficient and prompt completion. An experienced earth sheltered builder has the same advantage, especially if he is working from plans drawn by an experienced designer.

A preconstruction conference among the owner, architect, engineer, and contractor can help eliminate potential difficulties on the site, particularly if earth sheltering is new to the contractor. For the owner, who is likeliest of all to be new to earth sheltering, it will be a very educational experience. Come with your own list of questions arising from the contract documents. As the plans, specifications, and scheduling are discussed and critical steps rehearsed, take notes for your personal use during future property inspections. Make sure that any details left unspecified in contract documents are discussed.

Steps in a Sample Project

To demystify the process and illustrate the sequence of steps, an example of the building process followed on a particular house is given. Understanding the timing of each step in the sample project's completion will help you evaluate the construction schedule for your own job and pinpoint the times you want to be on-site.

The sample house features a combination of reinforced concrete block and poured-in-place and precast concrete; naturally, the use of different

Preparing to Monitor Construction Progress

Working from your discussions with the professionals and from the documents, prepare a checklist of the sequence of construction steps. Such a personal schedule will not only help you mentally organize and understand your project's progress, it will also help you to anticipate when and what to watch for on the site.

Depending on how compulsive you are, you may wish to enter considerable detail describing specific items to investigate. Checking off steps as they are completed to your satisfaction and that of your architect will assure you that scheduled payments are legitimately due.

Go over the checklist with your architect; he may have additional suggestions. This would be a good time to check signals as to when he will be on-site himself. A form for your checklist is suggested in the following worksheet; it is organized to correspond to the phases of construction for the sample project described in the following section.

	Materials/ Process Notes	Architect observes?	Date planned	Problems Noted	Date done to satisfaction
Site work: staking, clearing excavation					
Footings:					
Rough shell: walls, exterior walls, interior bearing intermediate floor roof deck retaining walls front window walls					
External finishing: parapet topping slab waterproofing insulation drain tile backfill					
Internal work: floor slab nonbearing partitions electrical, mechanical, and plumbing finishing interior					
Landscape work: contouring planting					

structural systems (post-tensioned concrete or wood, for example) would alter the sequence and duration of tasks.

The house used in this example is in a suburb of the Twin Cities. The designer is Eduardo Romo of Northeast Homeplanning and Design, New Brighton, Minnesota; the consulting engineer is Brent Anderson of Division 7 Corporation, Bloomington, Minnesota; and the project coordinator is Thomas Sopoci, architect. The time allotted for each step assumes an experienced crew of four or five workers. For an inexperienced contractor or a smaller crew, the times could triple.

Site Work
(Total time: two days)

Staking and Clearing: Since the misplacement of your house on the site is one construction error that cannot be corrected, you or your architect should be around for this step. After the outlines of the house are visible, trees will be marked for removal. Those within fifteen feet of the future walls will probably have to go to allow for a wide enough excavation area for work on walls from the outside.

Excavation: Depending on the equipment used, this process could take anywhere from four hours to two days. A large machine like a front-end loader, although more costly per hour than a smaller backhoe, can usually do the job far more quickly and thus less expensively in the long run.

Footings
(Total time: two days)
Footings are horizontal pads of concrete that bear and spread the weight of the structure. They are often, as in our example, reinforced with steel bars. The placement and tying together of these bars could well be checked before the concrete is poured.

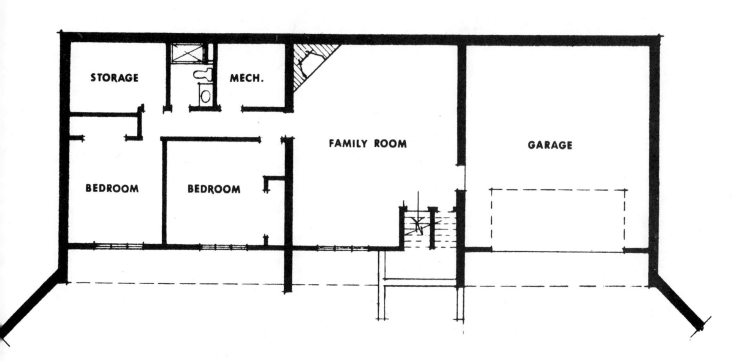

LOWER LEVEL PLAN

(Drawing courtesy of Eduardo Romo)

10—1. Floor plan (lower level) of a similar house to the one used in the sample construction process, different only in that the stairway is located at the front, whereas the sample house has the stairway (and consequently the footings to bear two stories of weight) at the back.

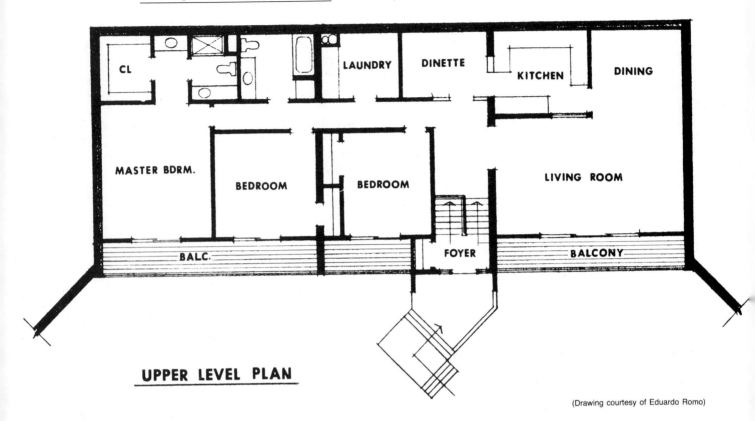

UPPER LEVEL PLAN

(Drawing courtesy of Eduardo Romo)

10–2. Plan of the upper level of the same house. Eduardo Romo is the designer of both the above house and our sample house.

10–3. The floor plans shown in figures 10–1 and 10–2 are actually for this house, designed by Eduardo Romo several years before our sample house was built. A different location of the entry and internal staircase, as well as the use of stucco as a facing instead of cedar, make the two finished houses look quite different from one another.

(Photo courtesy of Eduardo Romo)

10—4. Completed excavation in which the house will be built. Access by heavy equipment is not a problem on this suburban lot.

10–5. Forms are constructed for poured concrete footings. Load-bearing walls will rest on these footings. Reinforcing bars will be placed within the forms so that the concrete can be poured around them.

10—6. Completed footings look like this after the concrete has been poured and allowed to set and the forms have been removed. Vertical reinforcing bars have been placed at close intervals to tie the poured walls into the footings.

Rough Shell
(Total time: fifteen days for two-story structure)

Walls: The exterior walls in this two-story house are to be cast-in-place concrete. The wall forms for the first story are set up first, starting with the outside form.

Before the inside form is set up, reinforcing steel is placed, and rough openings for any electrical or plumbing lines will be formed. To the extent that any lines will be inside the wall, the inspector must check the work prior to the pouring. The architect or engineer should check the walls prior to and during the pour; you will find the process interesting to observe.

Constructing walls, from erection of forms through the finished pour, can take anywhere from a few days to about a week, depending on the size and shape of the house. The lower- and upper-story sets of walls, which are poured separately, each took five days on the sample house.

Roof Deck: The roof (or an intermediate floor, as in figure 10-10) is the next step toward completing the rough shell. Both roof deck and intermediate floor in this design will be precast concrete planks, which are supported by the three exterior poured walls and the two interior bearing walls of reinforced concrete block.

A precast concrete plank roof should take two or three days to complete. When the roof has been placed, a careful check of the whole shell should be made for cracking or deflection from shrinkage or shifting.

10—7. Reinforcing steel of the specified size has been placed and tied. The inside wall form is being set up, enclosing the steel inside the space into which the concrete will be poured.

10—8. The concrete truck arrives, the concrete is tested for proper mix and consistency, and the pouring begins. The 2 × 4s provide internal bracing; also visible are the internal load-bearing partitions, which are constructed of reinforced concrete block.

10—9. Pouring the concrete.

10—10. Precast hollow-core concrete planks have been lifted into place for the floor of the second story. The opening at the back is for the stairway. Vertical reinforcing is in place to connect into the second-story wall, which will be formed and poured next.

10—11. On the roof of the upper story, joints between the precast planks are filled with a sand/cement grout.

10–12. The nearly completed shell, showing roof, intermediate floor, poured exterior walls, and interior load-bearing walls of concrete block.

10-13. The parapet wall is being completed. Before the final course of block is placed on top, concrete is poured into the interior of the blocks to strengthen the parapet.

External Finishing
(Total time: four to six days)

Roof Parapet and Topping Slab: In this design, as in many you will encounter, a low wall is constructed along the entire front edge of the roof. Called a *parapet*, this reinforced concrete block wall acts like a retaining wall to contain the earth that will later be placed on the roof. The parapet also visually marks the front edge of the roof. A building codes official or your own prudence might suggest a higher physical barrier along the parapet (bushes or a fence) to prevent people from falling over the edge.

When the parapet and any roof penetrations (chimney and vent stacks in this design) have been completed, a thin layer of concrete is applied over the roof planks. This *topping slab* provides a smoothly finished surface for waterproofing. It is a 4-inch thick layer at the front (the inside base of the parapet),

and gradually thins to 2 inches at the back. The gentle slope will allow a soaking rain to drain off the back edge of the roof rather than pooling in the soil just above the roof's waterproof membrane.

Front (South) Wall: In this design the front wall with its large openings for windows is not concrete, except for the lower part, which is reinforced concrete block (see fig. 10-8) and will be partially buried. Called a *grade beam*, this lower portion of the front wall provides frost protection and will support the wood structure of the above-ground portions of the front wall.

The wall is recessed so that the roof and side walls both function as overhangs, protecting the south glass in the summer from the high noon sun and the lower morning and afternoon sun. The design steps back several feet on the eastern part of the facade—this also shades some of the windows on summer afternoons.

10—14. The topping slab is applied and carefully troweled. This slab has a 2-inch slope from front to back.

10—15. The finished roof deck, with the parapet wall on the left and the topping slab finished.

10—16. The front wall is being built using frame construction. The winter sun, being low, bypasses the overhang and strikes the entire glass area of each window.

Retaining Walls: The retaining wall, particularly on the east where two stories' worth of earth are being held back, must be very strong. Footings are formed and poured to supply a sturdy base, and then construction of forms for the poured-in-place retaining walls begins. The retaining wall will be reinforced with steel (see fig. 10-17) just as the walls of the house itself are.

Waterproofing: Products used to waterproof earth sheltered buildings come in various forms: there are roll or sheet products, some products are troweled on, and some are sprayed. Often a different product will be used for a horizontal application (the roof) than for the vertical surfaces of walls. None will work effectively unless applied according to the manufacturer's instructions. Now is a good time to be looking over your contractor's shoulder.

Insulation: Rigid insulation is placed over the waterproofing skin. Joints should be fitted tightly and staggered from layer to layer.

Backfill: Replacing earth around and over the house takes place as soon after waterproofing and insulation as possible. Make sure that walls are braced from the inside and that permeable soil is distributed evenly in tamped layers around the exterior. During the course of backfilling, drain tiles are laid down horizontally: one row may go in the soil around the outside of the walls at the same level as the footings, and another row may be placed nearer the surface.

Several different layers of soil are spread on the roof, including at least porous sand or a gravel layer for drainage and the specified soil required for the chosen plant types. At least twelve inches of soil is needed to support vegetation; for many climates and plants, depths up to twenty-four inches will be required. If heavy equipment is used to backfill the roof, the weight of the equipment should have been planned for when the roof loading was calculated.

When the shell is complete and covered, you can heave a sigh of relief; the most critical structural work has been done. It would be prudent, however much you trust your architect, engineer, and contractor, to make a comprehensive check for possible leaks after the next rainstorm.

10—17. With the front form not yet in place, the reinforcing steel for the lower portion of the east retaining wall is visible.

10—18. The finished retaining wall. Notice the pilasters (lower buttresslike walls extending back at 45-degree angles to the retaining wall); they add the stability needed by a retaining wall of this height. The thermal break (a slightly dark strip of insulation running vertically between the house wall and the retaining wall) prevents heat from being "wicked" out through the concrete to the exterior.

10–19. Bentonite, the waterproofing material being sprayed on the outside of the concrete walls, is actually a clay. Like many clays, bentonite expands when wet, so it can bridge small cracks or widened joints between concrete structural members.

10–20. Waterproofing the roof of this house involves the use of several products. EPDM, a synthetic rubber compound of the vulcanate group of products, comes in sheets and is being used in critical spots (over joints between roof planks in this photo) for extra protection. It will also be used as flashing on the inside of the parapet and around roof penetrations. Bentonite is sprayed over the EPDM and then over the entire roof surface.

10–21. Insulation is applied over the waterproof membrane (sprayed bentonite), which has been protected with a layer of cross-laminated polyethylene sheeting. Earth is then replaced directly over the insulation.

10-22. Backfilling is nearly complete.

Internal Work
(Total time: thirty to forty-five days)

Floor Slab: Any heating, electrical, or plumbing systems penetrating the floor must be completed before the slab is poured. Insulation may also be laid under the floor prior to pouring.

Partitions: Once the floor is poured, non-load-bearing partition walls can be constructed. Where their tops meet the ceiling, a half-inch or so of space (hidden by decorative finish later) may be left to allow for some downward deflection of the roof planks. Inspect to see if the walls are straight and corners square so cabinetry will fit properly.

Finishing: Cabinetry, appliances, light fixtures, hardware, and floor coverings are now installed. Though this work is not critical to the structure, it is to the functioning of the house.

As in any new house, a thousand details must be checked. In particular, test any equipment such as a wood-burning stove, furnace, or solar water heater by running it through a working cycle. Learn how to operate it and where to get it repaired. Make sure you receive from the supplier any pertinent warranties or guarantees.

Landscape Work
(Total time: two or three days)

As soon as water, gas, and sewer or septic systems are in and all other need for heavy equipment is over, the land surface can be contoured properly for drainage away from the house. The subcontractor (usually a nursery) plants the specified trees, shrubs, and grasses, arriving as soon as possible to prevent erosion of the soil.

Roof plantings are not limited to grass. Self-seeded native wild plants, rock gardens, drought-tolerant vines or ground covers, and even flower or vegetable gardens are among your possible choices. Since the roof is designed to drain water quickly, however, frequent irrigation and/or a good mulch are often necessary.

10—23. Interior stud walls are being built.

10–24. Landscape work in this design includes building a wood retaining wall on the west end of the house, pouring a driveway, and planting sod and trees.

Completion and Final Inspection

If there are no significant pauses in construction, you can anticipate that the total building period will take approximately three months. This period may lengthen, however, depending on the weather, the season when construction begins, and the extent to which you are participating in the finishing work.

10—25. A very generalized time line, from start to finish, for having an earth sheltered home built.

Final Inspection

Your acceptance of the house is formalized by your final payment to the contractor. Final inspections by you, your architect, the building codes official, and your lender's appraiser should all precede your acceptance.

What should you look for in your final inspection? First, remember that your best opportunities for detecting problems occur *during* construction. Most of the critical structural and waterproofing details have now been covered up. If there are still problems with these, they may not crop up for weeks, months, or even years.

Second, be guided by your architect.

Third, make a list, at home, of the items to check when you arrive for your final assessment. Work from checklists you used during construction.

You will be concentrating on finishing items that are not so different from those in a conventional house. The items peculiar to earth sheltering that you might catch and have corrected before acceptance are mainly leaks and cracks, which of course you have been watching for all along.

Assuming your final inspection indicates the building is substantially complete (your architect's advice on this point is part of his service), there remain possibly two other officials who must concur: the building inspector and the appraiser. When they are satisfied, the final payment can be made to the contractor, you can receive any warranties or guarantees that are forthcoming from him, make the final arrangements with your lender, and call the moving company.

Summary Time Line for the Entire Project

Although construction may only take three months, it should be evident from the previous chapters that the entire process could take much longer. If you choose the custom-designed, custom-built approach outlined in this book and do a thorough job of research and preparation, the project is likely to take a year.

Using standard plans from an earth sheltered building company, supplier, or other source will shorten the endeavor. If you must, you could always hire the right professionals and let them take care of everything. This would significantly reduce the amount of time you as an owner need to spend.

The actual level of involvement is up to you. Our intent has been to lay out all the alternatives but to argue for fully utilizing the strengths of everyone on your team. This means taxing yourself to do the things you can do the best: evaluate sites and designs—and professional skills—in the context of your own inclinations. It means tapping the experience and intuition of trained professionals to do what they do best.

The result should be a durable, lovely, and efficient home that responds appropriately to the climate it inhabits, the site it improves, and the owner it reflects. Good luck.

Chapter 11

Assessing an Existing Earth Sheltered Home

When most of us want to acquire a new conventional home, we find it much quicker to buy an existing home than to build one. Most of the defects in a conventional house are reasonably discernible to average consumers.

Buying an existing earth sheltered house is a different story altogether. Since earth sheltered houses are so new, few have appeared on the market for resale. It is estimated, however, that somewhere in the neighborhood of five to six thousand homes had been built by 1982. In addition, some speculation homes are always on the market. In the future, then, consumers may increasingly enjoy the option of buying rather than building an earth sheltered home.

If you should find an earth sheltered home that is for sale at the right price and quite fits your needs, how do you judge the soundness of its construction? What should you look for in any earth sheltered home you tour?

Structural Soundness and Waterproofing

There is no way to probe inside the walls to inspect steel placement or even to ascertain whether the waterproofing system is intact on buried surfaces. Evidence of problems can often be observed in other ways, however.

Interior
Look inside the house for these signs of leakage or structural problems:

- Cracks in the walls are extremely difficult to hide, even with patching. Cracks could mean a ruptured waterproofing membrane and present or future leaks; they could also indicate uneven settlement of the building or excessive deflection of the roof deck.
- Water stains or moldy smells could signify leaks.
- The insides of ducts may feel wet or slimy; check by lifting off grilles that cover duct openings and reaching in.

Exterior
On the outside of the house and up on the roof, look for these clues:

- Settlement or ponding water could indicate poorly compacted backfill or inadequate drainage.

- The condition of detailing at the edge of the parapet and around roof penetrations could indicate problems. Is the flashing exposed? In bad condition? Is any waterproofing material exposed?
- Are retaining walls in good condition? Is there any deflection outward?
- Is there fencing or planting along the roof edge to mark it? A potential liability problem exists if the drop over the front is not protected.
- Is any information available concerning the type of subsoil the house was built in and the level of the water table? Does the owner know?

Heating and Cooling Systems

If there is an active or passive solar heating system, find out how it works. Has the system met the owner's expectations? Does it require frequent manipulation or repair?

Be particularly watchful of a wood- or coal-burning stove: was it inspected when installed for proper distances from combustible surfaces, adequate insulation protection, and proper air intake and venting? Be sure the chimney stack is self-supporting and not holding any other weight.

Code Compliance

Here is where the real purpose of building codes can be put to work for you. Your protection as a second owner, with no control over the initial design and construction, is better assured if codes were met originally. If no codes are in effect for the area, the use of an architect or reputable builder would reduce your concern. Check the following:

- Fire safety would suggest two building exits, one remote from the other. Bedrooms should have a means of exit other than the door. There should be two smoke detectors, one in the sleeping area and one in the cooking area. To alleviate the hazards from interior fire (from kitchens, overstuffed chairs, drapes), adequate ventilation systems to vent smoke and/or poisonous gases would be desirable. Can firemen get in quickly?
- Electrical wiring should have been done according to codes; there is no reason for installations and connections to have been made any

less correctly than in above-ground homes. Ask who did the wiring: if the owner did, was it inspected? Bring in your own expert if you have any doubts.
- Air supply and ventilation in a very tightly enclosed structure must have been provided. How will the use of kerosene heaters or fireplaces affect the fresh-air supply? Supplemental or combustion air may be supplied, but check if it is enough. The two air changes per hour specified in the code implies lots of outside air bringing in possibly unfriendly temperatures. Perhaps a stategy for tempering it is available (an air-to-air heat exchanger, for example). Wet rot around windows or condensation collecting on the interior surface of skylights indicate inadequate ventilation of interior humidity.

Questions to Current Owner

- What have the backup utility or heating bills been?
- Have there been any leaks?
- Who designed the house?
- Who built the house? The owners themselves? A reputable contractor?
- Was a soils test done originally, so that the resulting information on bearing capacity could guide the engineering of the design?
- Were there any problems insuring the home?
- What other problems have there been?
- Why are you moving?

Suggested Conditions for Purchase

The insurance question raises an interesting fact about many earth sheltered houses. Some earth sheltered building companies and owners report that they have been able to negotiate lower insurance premiums than would be paid for similar but conventional homes, because the structure is less vulnerable to fire and storm damage. Several insurance firms have even announced lower rates, usually on condition that the home was designed by a qualified professional. When inspecting a house for potential purchase, ask whether the plans for the house had an engineer's stamp of approval. Buying a structure that was not professionally engineered could be a risky business.

The National Association of Mutual Insurance Companies (NAMIC) has circulated a list of areas for concern to insurance inspectors considering the underwriting of an earth sheltered home. NAMIC concluded that, assuming specific areas of concern are found to be satisfactory, earth sheltering is "an insurable risk" if the following conditions are met:

(1) the shelter is designed by an architect;
(2) the plans are checked and an engineer's stamp of approval is included;
(3) building codes are followed and quality building materials are used by a reputable qualified contractor;
(4) natural drainage and water table height are adequately determined;
(5) the foundation drainage is properly installed;
(6) good waterproofing material is expertly applied; and
(7) the supplemental heat (wood/coal burner) is properly installed (air intake and venting). Adequate clearance between heating devices and combustible materials must be maintained.

These conditions are sensible ones for a potential buyer to investigate before making a decision.

A design professional may be more astute in spotting trouble than a potential first-time earth sheltered homeowner. Consider hiring an experienced earth sheltered architect or engineer to inspect the property for a couple of hours. Most professionals will charge an hourly fee for such a service; it will be cheap insurance against a possible $100,000 mistake.

Finally, do not rush into this "readymade" decision any more quickly than you would leap into building a new home. Be sure this earth sheltered house fits your program, is truly as energy efficient as its owner or builder claims it is, appeals to your sense of aesthetics, and is located where you want to live. Compromise, of course, but remember that you have the knowledge to have your dream house built if you still feel that is the better choice.

Further Reading

Periodicals

Alternative Sources of Energy. Route 2, Box 90A, Milaca, MN 56353. Bimonthly

Earth Shelter Living (formerly *Earth Shelter Digest and Energy Report*). Webco Publishing, Inc., 1701 East Cope, St. Paul, MN 55109. Bimonthly.

New Shelter. Rodale Press, Emmaus, PA 18049. Bimonthly.

Underground Space. Pergamon Press, Maxwell House, Fairview Park, Elmsford, NY 10523. Bimonthly journal of the American Underground-Space Association (AUA).

Underline. Underground Space Center, University of Minnesota, 790 CME, 500 Pillsbury Drive, S. E., Minneapolis, MN 55455. Quarterly.

Books, Reports, Pamphlets

Barker, Michael. *Building Underground for People: Eleven Selected Projects in the U.S.* Washington, DC: American Institute of Architects, 1978.

Campbell, Stu. *The Underground House Book.* Charlotte, VT: Garden Way Publishing, 1980.

Center for Natural Energy Design. *Earth Sheltered Structures Fact Sheets.* Numbers 7–12 of a series of twelve prepared for the U.S. Department of Energy. Oklahoma State University, 1981.
  07—"Daylighting Design"
  08—"Indoor Air Quality"
  09—"Earth Coupled Cooling Techniques"
  10—"Disaster Protection"
  11—"Building in Expansive Clays"
  12—"Passive Solar Heating"
  Available from Underground Space Center, University of Minnesota; Center for Natural Energy Design, Oklahoma State University; and American Underground-Space Association (see Appendix B).

Frenette, Edward R., and Holthusen, T. Lance, eds. *Earth Sheltering: The Form of Energy and the Energy of Form.* Elmsford, NY: Pergamon Press, 1981.
  This 250-page book, introduced by Frenette's thoughtful essay on current architectural responses to energy conservation, features fifty award-winning and exemplary designs from the American Underground-Space Association (AUA) 1980–81 Design Competition. State-of-the-art underground design work, impressive and creative, is presented in the context of careful judgment and evaluation. Available from AUA (see Appendix B).

Holthusen, T. Lance. ed. *The Potential of Earth-Sheltered and Underground Space: Today's Resource for Tomorrow's Space and Energy Viability.* Elmsford, NY: Pergamon Press, 1981.

147

This 500-page volume of proceedings includes forty-two papers presented at AUA's Underground Space Conference and Exposition in Kansas City, June, 1981. It comprises a good overview of the status of earth sheltered building, public policy, urban underground planning, and deep underground space use, and is available from AUA (see Appendix B).

Labs, Kenneth. *A Regional Analysis of Ground and Above Ground Climate*. Washington DC: (Research sponsored by) U.S. Department of Energy, 1981.

In this 192-page study, Labs discusses the regional suitability of underground construction with reference to an analysis of weather data around the United States, data bases of synthesized ground temperatures in the United States, and monthly dew point temperature comparisons for identifying relative potentials for condensation in various regions. The study is available from AUA (see Appendix B).

Mazria, Edward. *The Passive Solar Energy Book: A Complete Guide to Passive Solar Home, Greenhouse and Building Design*. Emmaus, PA: Rodale Press, 1979. (An Expanded Professional Edition is also available.)

National Association of Mutual Insurance Companies. *NAMIC Energy Bulletin*. Indianapolis, IN: National Association of Mutual Insurance Companies, 1981.

Oehler, Mike. *The $50 and Up Underground House Book*. 4th ed. New York: Van Nostrand Reinhold Company Inc., 1981.

Roy Robert L. *Underground Houses: How to Build a Low Cost Home*. New York: Sterling Publishing Company, Inc., 1979.

A book for do-it-yourselfers, this is an easy-to-follow guide to the process of building inexpensive but efficient structures. It is available in bookstores or from the publisher. Our quote in chapter 5 actually comes from a paper Mr. Roy presented at an Underground Space Center conference and exhibition on earth sheltering in 1980. Mr. Roy's and nineteen other interesting papers, both technical and practical, are in *Collected Papers Presented at: Earth Sheltered Housing Conference & Exhibition—1*, available from the Underground Space Center.

Setter, Leach & Lindstrom, Inc. *Earth Sheltered Construction*. Photocopy report, results of study done with the assistance of the Underground Space Center for the U.S. Navy.

Extensive computer analysis of various climates, building shapes, and levels of earth cover resulted in information that will help designers plan, design, and construct buildings appropriately for optimum energy economy in different climates.

Shurcliff, William A. *Super Insulated Homes and Double Envelope Houses*. Andover, MA: Brick House Publishing Company, 1981.

Tatum, Rita. *The Alternative House: A Complete Guide to Building and Buying*. Los Angeles: Reed Books (division of Addison House), 1978.

Underground Space Center, University of Minnesota. *Earth Sheltered Housing: Code, Zoning, and Finance Issues*. New York: Van Nostrand Reinhold Company Inc., 1981.

An exploration of potential obstacles to the spread of earth sheltering and recommendations of ways to remove such obstacles where possible.

Underground Space Center, University of Minnesota. *Earth Sheltered Homes: Plans and Designs*. New York: Van Nostrand Reinhold Company Inc., 1981.

This is a picture book showing color photos, floor plans, and brief descriptions of some of the best earth sheltered homes in the country. If nothing has convinced you so far that an earth sheltered house is not a cave, get this book. Available in bookstores or from the publishers.

Underground Space Center, University of Minnesota. *Earth Sheltered Housing Design: Guidelines, Examples, and References*. New York: Van Nostrand Reinhold Company Inc., 1978.

Since its original publication, this 318-page report has sold several hundred thousand copies, with good reason. If by chance you have not seen it, look in bookstores, order it from the publisher or from AUA. Quite technical and detailed about design issues, nevertheless it is clear and readable as well as encyclopedic. You will refer to it over and over.

Underground Space Center, University of Minnesota, *Earth Sheltered Residential Design Manual*. New York: Van Nostrand Reinhold Company Inc., 1982.

This is a 252-page follow-up to *Earth Sheltered Housing Design*. It incorporates new and more specific design information based on the research and practical experience gained by the Underground Space Center staff, including complete coverage of insulation, waterproofing, soils, structural systems, and landscaping.

Underground Space Center, University of Minnesota. *Earth Sheltered Structures Fact Sheets*. Washington, DC: Numbers 1–6 of a series of twelve prepared for the U.S. Department of Energy.

01—"Site Investigation"
02—"Planting Considerations"
03—"Waterproofing Techniques"
04—"Waterproofing Considerations and Materials"
05—"Insulation Principles"
06—"Insulation Materials and Placement"
Available from Underground Space Center, University of Minnesota; Center for Natural Energy Design, Oklahoma State University; and American Underground-Space Association (see Appendix B).

Waschek, Carmen and Brownlee. *Your Guide to Good Shelter: How to Plan, Build or Convert for Energy Conservation*. Reston, VA: Prentice-Hall, Reston Publishing Company, Inc., 1978.

Wells, Malcolm. *Underground Designs*. Brewster, MA: Malcolm Wells, 1977.

Filled with illustrations of many details and designs, including eighteen home designs, this is a valuable idea book. Short sections deal with selecting a site, structural choices, code problems, waterproofing, insulation, and landscaping. The eighty-seven page book is available from the author, for $6.00 postpaid, at Box 1149, Brewster, MA 02631.

Wells, Malcolm, and Glenn-Wells, Sam. *Underground Plans Book—1*. Brewster, MA: Malcolm Wells, 1980.

Forty-four very large pages show large-scale floor plans, cross-sections, elevations, perspectives, and details of eight home designs, including "House for a North Slope." With these 1/4-inch scale drawings, you or your designer or builder can produce the drawings needed for your own house.

Available for $13.00 postpaid from Malcolm Wells, Box 1149, Brewster, MA 02631.

Wright, David. *Natural Solar Architecture: A Passive Primer*. Rev. ed. New York: Van Nostrand Reinhold Company Inc., 1978.

Wright, David, and Andrejko, Dennis. *Passive Solar Architecture: Logic and Beauty*. New York: Van Nostrand Reinhold Company Inc., 1982.

Research and Information Centers

American Underground-Space Association
790 CME
500 Pillsbury Drive, S.E.
Minneapolis, MN 55455
(612)376-5580

Center for Natural Energy Design
School of Architecture
Division of Engineering
Oklahoma State University
Stillwater, OK 74078
(405)624-6266

Conservation and Renewable Energy Inquiry and Referral Service (CAREIRS)
(formerly National Solar Heating and Cooling Information Center)
P.O. Box 8900
Silver Springs, MD 20907
(800)523-2929

Underground Space Center
790 CME
500 Pillsbury Drive, S.E.
University of Minnesota
Minneapolis, MN 55455
(612)376-5341

Earth Sheltered Design Resources

Surveying the variety of forms earth sheltered design can take will stimulate your imagination and introduce you to the range of variation available. There are three kinds of resources you can investigate.

First, a growing body of publications are devoted specifically to describing earth sheltering by means of specific plans, designs, photographs, and descriptions. Second, many earth sheltered designers and/or builders privately offer descriptive booklets or brochures that describe the stock or predesigned plans they offer for sale. Third, you can use the *Reader's Guide to Periodical Literature* in the library. Many popular and professional magazines in the last five years have published articles about earth sheltering, and most show photographs and floor plans of exemplary houses. At any given time there is likely to be at least one general home design magazine on the current racks that features an earth sheltered design or two.

Another good resource is *Earth Shelter Living*, formerly *Earth Shelter Digest and Energy Report*, a bimonthly magazine published by Webco Publishing, Inc., 1701 East Cope, St. Paul, MN 55109. Every issue contains several case studies of built houses, including owner or designer descriptions, floor plans, and photographs.

Publications of Plans and Designs

Design Concept Associates. *Homes in the Earth*. San Francisco: Chronicle Books, 1980.

Frenette, Edward R., and Holthusen, T. Lance, eds. *Earth Sheltering: The Form of Energy and the Energy of Form*. Elmsford, NY: Pergamon Press, 1981.

Langley, John. *Sun Belt Earth Sheltered Architecture*. Winter Park, FL: John Langley, 1979. (Available from John Langley, P.O. Box 729, Winter Park, FL 32790.

Underground Space Center, University of Minnesota. Earth Sheltered Homes: Plans and Designs. New York: Van Nostrand Reinhold Company Inc., 1981.

Wells, Malcolm. *Underground Designs*. Brewster, MA: Malcolm Wells, $6.00 postpaid from Malcolm Wells, P.O. Box 1149, Brewster, MA 02631.)

Wells, Malcolm, and Glenn-Wells, Sam. *Underground Plans Book—1*. 1980. ($13.00 postpaid from Malcolm Wells, P.O. Box 1149, Brewster, MA 02631.)

Sources of Predesigned Plans

The following earth sheltered designers and/or builders offer books or brochures, either free or at a small cost. These pieces illustrate and describe plans for which the full working drawings can be either purchased or used in combination with construction services.

Many architects around the country have produced designs for several custom earth sheltered houses and seen them built—some have done many more. It is neither possible nor politic to try to list them all.

The architects listed below as providing stock plans also do custom work, but to find a custom designer with experience, it is probably best to investigate first the local and then the national sources mentioned in chapter 5. There are advantages in working with a local expert who is intimately familiar with your own climate, soils, and codes, and with whom you can consult closely and often.

Alternative Housing Institute, Casas Adobes Station, P.O. Box 35926, Tucson, AZ 85740.

The Institute offers a wide range of services, including seminars on earth sheltering and a mail-order bookstore of earth sheltered and solar books. Stock house plans are also available, as are design and construction supervision services.

Architerra, Inc., Rosslyn Center, 1700 North Moore Street, Arlington, VA 22209.

Architerra, Inc. is a planning and design firm. It combines its architectural capabilities and expertise with an associated soils engineering technology resulting in the efficient use of land by stabilizing slopes that might otherwise be too steep for economical development. Architerra assists professionals in applying its systems through feasibility studies and cost estimates, site planning, drawings, and specifications, and on-site construction supervision. A packet of descriptive information is available.

John E. Barnard, Jr., AIA, Race Lane, Marston Mills, MA 02648.

Mr. Barnard's "Ecology House," an atrium type of design completed in 1973, has been published widely. In addition to custom architectural services, he offers stock one-, two-, and three-bedroom plans that include both atrium and elevation styles. A brochure describing the plans is available.

Berg & Associates, Design/Build, Inc., 3140 Harbor Lane, Plymouth, MN 55441.

This design/build architecture firm offers complete architectural and engineering services, including consulting, bidding and construction inspection/supervision; site planning and site selection consulting; and construction services, including construction management, complete general contracting or special subcontracting. While most work is commissioned on a custom basis, a standard plan catalog is available.

Betterway Underground Homes, P.O. Box 825, Kansas City, MO 64141.

"It has been a long, bitter winter. You and your friend return from a business trip to find the power has been off for two days. His family has moved in with the in-laws. His pipes are frozen and broken. You walk into your home, greet your family, hang up your coat, roll up your sleeves, and sit down in front of your fireplace to a warm evening meal. You live in an underground home." The services provided by this company include the sale of standard plans (each introduced by a piece like the one quoted above), as well as custom design

services. A descriptive booklet of the plans offered is available.

Colorado Sunworks, P.O. Box 455, Boulder, CO 80306.

This firm markets the plans for one house, and it is a good one. Called The SunEarth House, the original was built in 1978. It is 100 percent independent of fossil fuel for heat; 5.8 percent of the heat used is supplied by a fireplace, 17.2 percent by lights, appliances, people, etc., and 77 percent by passive solar. Consulting is available for design and construction. A four-page brochure describes the design.

Davis Caves, Inc., Box 102, Armington, IL 61721.

This construction company will send crews anywhere in the United States to build just the concrete shell or the complete home. Customer may choose from a number of pre-engineered designs. A color brochure showing floor plans and photographs of finished homes is available.

Earthborne Construction, Inc., Route 1, Marshalltown, IA 50158.

A custom design and construction company, this firm offers no standard plans. Architectural and engineering services are available, of course; the company will also build just the rough shell, or its crews can complete the entire building.

Earth Shelter Corporation of America, Route 2, Box 97B, Berlin, WI 54923.

One of the first earth sheltered construction companies, Earth Shelter Corporation has a national network of franchised builders who work from a range of nearly twenty pre-engineered and certified plans. An architectural and engineering staff is available for adaptations or special situations, and the company can provide materials and application of a waterproofing system that it will then warrant for twenty years. A full-color brochure and also a color portfolio describing each design is available.

Earth Shelters Inc., P.O. Box 52, Omaha, NE 68101.

Services available from this firm include information, planning, consulting, custom design, and construction. A booklet of plans and drawings is available and is used as a starting point for custom-design services.

Earth Systems, Inc., P.O. Box 35338, Phoenix, AZ 85069.

This earth sheltered building company offers pre-engineered standard plans with professional engineering/drafting services available for custom designs. The company provides plans and also a kit of materials for domed structures. An illustrated booklet explains the system and the layouts and options available.

Everstrong Marketing, Inc., Box 431, Redwood Falls, MN 56283.

This firm builds earth sheltered homes of pressurized wood with 2×10 sidewall construction. Sidewalls are insulated to R-31, and the design includes a subfloor plenum with rock storage. The heating bill for the company's office (housed in their two-bedroom, 1,040-square-foot model) was $75 for 1980! Homes purchased from Everstrong can be built anywhere in the United States or Canada and carry a ten-year bonded warranty. Architectural services are available. A book describing the Everstrong plans may be obtained from the firm.

Don Metz, Architect, Lyme, NH.
Although he specializes in one-of-a-kind underground houses, Mr. Metz offers one ready-made set of plans for the Earthtech 6 House (shown in chapter 2). Descriptive brochure or the construction drawings are available through Garden Way Publishing Company, Charlotte, VT 05445.

The Outdoors People, 26600 Fallbrook Avenue, Wyoming, MN 55092.
An established dome home designing and building company with in-house architectural and engineering services and a national dealer network, this firm also offers standard plans for earth sheltered houses. In addition, T.O.P. provides such services as precut kit packages, partial or complete construction services, on-site supervision, and a school for owner-builders. A literature packet describing domed and earth sheltered plans is available.

Simmons & Sun, Inc.—Solar Earth Consultants, Inc., P.O. Box 1497, High Ridge, MO 63049
Using the technology of post-tensioning, this earth sheltered construction company/consulting firm offers numerous floor plans. In addition, it will supply materials to local contractors, men or crews to assist, or even complete construction services through its own crews or those of its local licensees. A full-color brochure and a seventy-page book of floor plans with brief discussions of codes, site selection, etc., are available.

Spatial Experiences, 912 Bell Ave., Denton, TX 76201.
This firm designs and builds, or assists owners in building, ferrocement structures. (These are thin-shelled curvilinear structures constructed of a special concrete mixture troweled onto a skeleton of reinforcing steel, metal lathe, and mesh that has been tied and laid over a plywood skin. The plywood is later removed from the interior, and the interior is plastered.) Plans can be purchased, but since the medium of ferrocement is so flexible, the firm has found that individual home owners usually like to tailor the structure to their desires. Personalized design help is available.

Sunpower Construction, 8975 Curtis Lake Road, Minocqua, WI 54548.
This general building contractor builds from several pre-engineered designs using poured and reinforced concrete walls, prestressed hollow-core concrete plank roof, and poured concrete wing walls. Standard features include completely engineered plans, either a greenhouse, sunspace, solarium, or atrium to bring a little sun into your life, and a lifetime warranty on the below-grade waterproofing system. Customer may choose to finish the interior. Book of plans are available.

Terra-Dome Corporation, 14 Oak Hill Cluster, Independence, MO 64050.
Through traveling work crews from the home office and through dealerships around the country, Terra-Dome offers a patented system for constructing modular earth sheltered structures. Architectural and engineering services are available, and company crews or dealers construct the basic structure. Two books are available: *Underground Design for Twenty-first Century Living* contains thirty-five floor plans and information on financing and planning an earth sheltered home, and *Twenty-first Century Homes* describes the modular construction and systems Terra-Dome uses.

TerraHab Company, P.O. Box 648, Plymouth, MI 48170.
This company's service is the sale of standard plans; the plans include drawings and specifications, guidelines for design alterations, suggestions for insulation and alternate energy sources, and a list of material sources. A booklet is available that includes renderings and floor plans for six designs.

Topic Earth Homes, P.O. Box 317, Shakopee, MN 55379.
The Topic House in Shakopee, built in 1976, is one of the earliest and most photographed earth sheltered houses. This is the house that, with all the electricity turned off except the refrigerator, never dropped below 40°F during the winter months the owners left it for warmer climates. Topic Earth Homes offers stock plans for sale, design services for modifications, and construction services. References and histories are available.

U'Bahn Earth Homes, Inc., P.O. Box 1026 NS, Granite City, IL 62040.
An underground home design company, U'Bahn offers blueprints for ten designs. In addition, consulting architectural and engineering staffs can modify the designs to suit a client, or problem-solve and produce final drawings for individuals who are designing their own homes. Components needed to construct U'Bahn homes (with the exception of the concrete) can be purchased. An illustrated floor plan book is available.

Underground Homes, R.R. 1, P.O. Box 160D, Wellsville, KS 66092.
The services this firm provides include planning services and the sale of blueprints for standard house plans. A book entitled *Go Underground and Save* is available.

Under-the-Earth Homes, Ltd., P.O. Box 38, Cable, WI 54821.
This is a custom design/build firm, offering construction services either for the rough shell or full buildings. Because of the warranty and insurance agreements provided, they do not offer partial service but build and warrant their own product. Local dealers are found in each area and assigned a dealer area; they build under Under-the-Earth's control. One of Under-the-Earth's homes is shown in chapter 5. There is a sample booklet of plans, renderings, and drawings available.

GLOSSARY

Active solar system. Any solar heating system that requires mechanical means, such as motors, pumps, or valves, to operate.

Adjustable rate mortgage (ARM). An alternative mortgage instrument in which the interest rate may be adjusted up or down after a specified time period, based on a lending institution's cost of funds. Sometimes called a Renegotiable Rate Mortgage (RRM).

Amortization. Gradual debt reduction. Normally, the reduction is made according to a predetermined schedule for installment payments.

Appraisal. A report made by a qualified person setting forth an opinion or estimate of value. The term also refers to the process by which this estimate is obtained.

Atrium. The main inner court of a Roman house, open to the sky and surrounded by the roof.

Atrium plan. An earth sheltered house design that features an internal courtyard. Atrium plans are often modified; sometimes the atrium is covered with glass rather than left open to the weather; sometimes the atrium becomes an entry courtyard and is surrounded on only three sides by the house.

Backfill. Soil replaced in an area that has been previously excavated. Backfill is used to fill the space between the excavation and the exterior of a structure, or around foundation walls to provide means for water to drain away. In earth sheltering, backfilling can also include the earth covering placed on a roof.

Backhoe. An excavating machine for cutting trenches. On this machine, a boom-mounted bucket moves toward the cab, cutting the ground like a hoe; then the machine turns away from the cut to permit the operator to dump the spoil.

Basement house. A house in which the living space consists entirely of what was intended to be only its basement. Common just after World War II, such houses featured a grade-level entry above the roof (the future first floor). Some basement houses remained unfinished for many years, and zoning ordinances prohibiting such eyesores were enacted in many communities.

Bearing capacity. The load per unit area that can be supported safely.

Bentonite. A clay, formed from decomposed volcanic ash, that can absorb a considerable amount of water, swelling accordingly.

Berm. A bank of earth, as the piled-up earth along a canal or against a masonry wall.

Boring. See Soil boring.

British thermal unit (Btu). The amount of heat required to raise one pound of water 1°F.

Btu. See British thermal unit.

Bubble diagram. A drawing that uses loose circles to show spaces that will be devoted to particular uses. Circles designating such uses as sleeping and eating can be rearranged easily in successive diagrams, allowing a designer to settle room relationships before drawing actual shapes and dimensions.

Building permit. A written authorization to an applicant (usually a builder) for a specific project, allowing construction to proceed. A building permit is granted by a municipal agency having jurisdiction after the building plans have been filed and reviewed for compliance with building codes or zoning ordinances.

Cast-in-place concrete. Concrete that is poured in the place where it is required, to harden as part of the structure (as opposed to precast concrete).

Caulking. A resilient mastic compound used to seal cracks, fill joints, prevent leakage, and/or provide waterproofing.

Change order. A written order to the contractor signed by the owner and the architect, issued after the execution of the contract, authorizing a change in the work or an adjustment in the contract sum or the contract time as originally defined by the contract documents. A change order may add to, subtract from, or vary the scope of the work.

Clerestory (or Clearstory). An upper zone of wall pierced with windows that admit light to a lofty room; or a window so placed.

Comparable. Meaning "comparable property," a recently sold property chosen for its similarity to one that is being appraised. Having an established market value, such a similar property is useful in estimating the value of a subject property. Comparables are structures of approximately the same size and location with similar amenities that have sold in the previous year.

Concrete. A mixture of portland cement, sand, and aggregate (crushed stone or gravel).

Conduction. The passage of electricity, sound, or heat through material. Thermal conduction is the process of heat transfer through a material medium in which kinetic energy is transmitted by particles of the material from particle to particle without gross displacement of the particles.

Construction loan. A short-term, interim loan for financing the cost of construction. The lender makes payments to the builder at periodic intervals as the work progresses.

Contingency allowance. A sum designated to cover unpredictable or unforeseen items of work or changes subsequently required by the owner.

Contour line. A line on a map or drawing connecting points of equal elevation on the ground.

Contract documents. Those documents that comprise a construction contract, including the owner-contractor agreement, conditions of the contract, plans and/or drawings, specifications, all addenda, and any modifications and changes thereto.

Convection. Heat transmission, either natural or forced (by means of a fan or pump), by currents of air or water. Such currents result from differences in density caused by temperature differences. Heat is transferred by the flow of its carrier.

Conventional loan. A mortgage loan neither insured by FHA nor guaranteed by VA.

Cross-section. See section.

Deflection. Any displacement in a body from its static position or from an established direction or plane as a result of forces acting on the body; or the deformation of a structural member as a result of loads acting on it.

Degree day. A unit of measurement used in estimating the fuel consumption for a building in a given climate. A degree day is equal to the number of degrees by which the mean temperature for a twenty-four-hour day differs from a "base temperature." The base temperature in the United States is 65°F for heating; 75°F for cooling.

Design development. The second phase of the architect's basic services. Following the presentation and owner acceptance of schematic design studies, the architect in this phase prepares more specific and detailed documents consisting of drawings and specifications to fix and describe the size and character of the project as to structural, mechanical and electrical systems, materials, and other essentials.

Direct gain system. The simplest and most frequently used approach to passive solar heating. Sunshine (solar gain) entering through windows is absorbed and stored within the space to be heated.

Drain tile. A hollow clay tile, usually laid end to end as piping (with open joints) in soil to drain water-saturated soil.

Egress. An exit or means of exiting.

Elevation. An external face of a building; or a drawing showing the vertical elements of a building, either exterior or interior, as a direct projection to a vertical plane.

Elevational plan. A type of design for an earth sheltered house that has only one elevation or face of the building exposed; the other sides are covered with earth.

EPDM. A synthetic rubber waterproofing compound that has been vulcanized and formed into a sheet membrane.

Expanded polystyrene. A foamed styrene plastic. Having high resistance to heat flow, expanded polystyrene (sometimes called beadboard) is often used as a rigid insulation product. Since it absorbs moisture more readily than extruded polystyrene, it is not as appropriate for use below grade because wetness reduces its insulating value.

Extruded polystyrene. A styrene plastic formed by forcing the material through a shaped opening. Used as rigid insulation, this product absorbs less moisture than expanded polystyrene and is more commonly used in below-grade situations.

Federal Home Loan Mortgage Corporation (FHLMC). A private corporation, authorized by Congress, that buys pools of mortgage loans and uses them to secure participation sales certificates. Popularly known as "Freddie Mac" or "The Mortgage Corp."

Federal Housing Administration (FHA). A division of the United States Department of Housing and Urban Development. It mainly insures residential mortgage loans made by private lenders. FHA does not lend money, nor plan, nor construct housing.

Federal National Mortgage Association (FNMA). A tax-paying corporation created by Congress to support the secondary mortgage market. It purchases and sells residential mortgages insured by FHA or guaranteed by VA, as well as conventional home mortgages. Popularly known as "Fannie Mae."

FHA. See Federal Housing Administration.

FHLMC. See Federal Home Loan Mortgage Corporation.

Flashing. A thin, impervious material placed to prevent water penetration and to weatherproof critical areas. Flashing may be used at the junction of two differing materials or at a joint between two structural elements such as a chimney and a roof, or a parapet wall and a roof.

FNMA. See Federal National Mortgage Association.

Footings. That portion of a foundation, wall, or column that transmits loads directly to the soil. Footings are wider than the walls they support in order to spread the load over a greater area, thus preventing or reducing settling.

Forms or Formwork. A temporary construction to contain wet concrete in the required shape while it is cast and cured.

Framing. A system of structural woodwork; or the rough timber structure of a building, such as partitions, flooring, and roofing.

Front-end loader. A bucket and lift-arm assembly designed for use on the front of a tractor. Unlike the backhoe, on which the boom-mounted bucket scoops backwards, the front-end loader scoops and lifts forward.

GPM. See Graduated payment mortgage.

Graduated payment mortgage (GPM). An amortized fixed-rate alternative mortgage instrument on which initial monthly payments are low and increase on a schedule based on the borrower's expected earnings increases and ability to pay.

Heat pump. A reversible system for extracting heat from a heat source and pumping it into a space when heating is required or, alternatively, for extracting heat from the space and storing or discharging it when cooling is required.

Heat loss. The speed and amount of heat transmitted through a given material. The heat loss of an entire house should be computed to determine the correct size of furnace or air-conditioning units.

Heat transfer. The movement of heat from a warmer to a cooler space. Heat transfers in three ways: through matter by conduction, from one body to another by radiation, and around spaces by being carried along with moving fluids such as water or air (convection).

Hollow-core plank. See Prestressed hollow-core plank.

Infiltration. A seepage or flow of air into a space through unintentional cracks such as those around windows and under doors.

Insolation. The rate at which energy from the sun reaches the earth's surface. Usually measured in Btu/sq.ft./day.

Insulation. Use of a nonconducting material to prevent passage of external heat from a body.

Interim financing. A short-term construction loan.

Lien. A right enforceable against specific property to secure payment of an obligation. A mechanic's lien is allowable under various state laws to protect persons supplying labor and/or materials for improvements on the specific property. Generally, the existence of an unsettled mechanic's lien prevents obtaining a clear title to the property.

Lien waiver. An instrument by which a person or organization having the right of mechanic's lien against the property of another relinquishes such a right.

Life-cycle costs. The entire cost of a structure during its expected term of use. In addition to the initial investment in land, design, and construction, life-cycle costs also include the periodic costs of financing, maintenance, repairs, and utilities. Since in recent years the ongoing costs to operate a structure have risen dramatically, the total life-cycle costs for a building, rather than construction costs alone, should be considered when choosing design and materials.

Load-bearing wall or partition. A wall or partition capable of supporting an imposed load in addition to its own weight.

Market comparable. See Comparable.

Market value. The highest price that a buyer, willing but not compelled to buy, would pay; and the lowest a seller, willing but not compelled to sell, would accept.

Masonry. That branch of construction dealing with plastering, concrete construction, and the shaping, arranging, and uniting of stone, brick, tile, and other such units with mortar.

Mass. A basic property of matter, for everyday purposes identical with weight. Massive materials include earth, stone, concrete, and water. The use of such materials for thermal mass is occasioned by their excellent capacity to absorb and store energy in the form of heat.

Mass wall. A wall intended for use as thermal storage. Made of a massive material such as masonry (Trombe wall) or water in containers (water wall), a mass wall is placed between south-facing glass and the space to be heated. Sunlight coming through the glass heats the wall's exterior surface. Heat is gradually conducted to the opposite side of the mass wall, from which it radiates to the living space.

Microclimate. The specific climatic characteristics present at an individual building site.

Minimum Property Standards (MPS). FHA regulations that set forth minimum acceptable technical standards for properties built or financed with the help of FHA or HUD programs.

Modified bitumens. A category of waterproofing material that comes in rolls and is adhered to the exterior structural surface. Modified bitumens are a combination of asphalt and synthetic rubber applied to a sheet of polyethylene.

Mortar. Material used to hold masonry together, made from portland cement, sand, and lime.

MPS. See Minimum Property Standards.

NAMIC. National Association of Mutual Insurance Companies.

Parapet. A low guarding or retaining wall at any point of sudden drop, as at the edge of a terrace, roof, or balcony.

Passive Solar System. As distinguished from an active solar system, a means of solar heating that requires little or no mechanical assistance to collect, store, and distribute heat from solar radiation into the space to be heated. With a passive system, the windows of the space are collectors, floor and wall surfaces and absorbers, and storage mass is incorporated into the structure's floors and walls.

Penetration. An opening through an exterior wall or roof of a structure to allow for a window, a door, a chimney, or a vent.

Penetrational plan. A type of design for an earth sheltered house that allows for openings or penetrations on otherwise earth-covered walls by means of retaining walls on either side of the opening to hold the earth back. The earth covering is thus "penetrated" wherever openings for windows or doors are called for in the design.

Percolation. Movement, under hydrostatic pressure, of water through the pores or spaces of rock or soil.

Permanent financing. A long-term mortgage loan.

Permeable. Porous enough to allow the passage of water and/or water vapor.

Perspective. The technique of representing solid objects on a flat surface so that they appear three-dimensional; or a picture or drawing employing this technique.

PITI. In mortgage lending, a shorthand for four factors: principal, interest, taxes, and insurance. These factors are used to compute the regular and predictable monthly expenses for a property being considered. The principal and interest payment on most loans is fixed for the term of the loan; the tax and insurance portion may be adjusted to reflect changes in taxes or insurance costs.

Portland cement. A generic product named for Portland, England, where it was developed. This product is a mixture of baked and ground limestone and cement, to which sand, aggregate, and water are added to make concrete.

Post-tensioning. A variation of prestressed concrete in which the reinforcing steel tendons are tensioned after the concrete has hardened.

Poured-in-place concrete. See Cast-in-place concrete.

Precast concrete. A concrete member such as a hollow-core plank or a panel that is cast and cured in other than its final position.

Precast concrete hollow-core plank. See Prestressed hollow core plank.

Precast concrete panel. An example of one of the shapes into which concrete is cast. Used extensively for walls in ordinary commercial construction, precast panels are normally 8 inches thick by 8 feet by the height specified in the design. For economy of materials, weight reduction, and strength, they are often pre-stressed and contain hollow cores. Under the right design conditions, panels for earth sheltered house shells can be used either vertically or horizontally, for load-bearing walls, or for roofs and/or intermediate floors.

Pressure-treated wood. Wood that has been treated with any of a variety of fungicides that are applied under pressure in order to allow deeper penetration. Wood that will come in contact with soil should always be pressure-treated to retard decay.

Prestressed concrete. A development of ordinary reinforced concrete. The reinforcing steel is replaced by wire cable in ducts. Compression is achieved by stretching the cables either before or after the casting of the concrete. Prestressed concrete is always used in precast forms (see also Prestressed hollow-core plant or Precast concrete panel).

Prestressed hollow-core plank. One of the precast shapes most commonly used in concrete earth sheltered houses. Looking and functioning somewhat like planks, they are normally 8 or 12 inches thick, 2 to 8 feet wide, and are sawed to the length appropriate to their strength and the span required. Voids or empty cores run longitudinally within the plank; they are sometimes used for air or utility ducts. Supported by load-bearing walls on each end, hollow-core planks are used to form intermediate floors or roof decks.

Primary lender. The financial institution from which the consumer secures a mortgage commitment. Primary lenders originate mortgages; investors in the secondary mortgage market may buy pools of mortgages originated by primary lenders.

Program. A statement prepared by or for an owner, with or without an architect's assistance, setting forth the conditions and objectives for a building project, including its general purpose and detailed requirements.

Radiation. The transmission of heat from a hot surface through space to a cooler one, in the form of invisible electromagnetic waves. The heat energy passes through the air between the source and the cooler body, being absorbed by the cooler surface and raising its temperature, without heating the intervening air appreciably.

Rebar. Shorthand for "reinforcing bar," a steel bar having ribs to provide greater bonding strength when used as a reinforcing bar in reinforced concrete.

Reinforced concrete block. Standard concrete blocks that are not individually reinforced but rather are strengthened collectively during or after laying up. Block walls can be reinforced vertically by means of pouring cement through and into their cores, and additionally by inserting reinforcing bars at regular intervals down through the cores.

Reinforcing bar. A steel bar used in concrete construction, for example, inside a poured concrete beam or wall, to provide additional strength.

Retaining wall. A wall, either freestanding or laterally braced, that bears against an earth or other fill surface and resists lateral and other forces from the material in contact with the side of the wall.

Rough shell. The essential structural elements of a building in their rough or unfinished state. The shell would include interior and exterior load-bearing walls, any intermediate floors, and roof.

Schematic drawings. Drawings prepared to illustrate the results of the first phase of the design process. These design studies show the scale as well as the relationships among the component parts of the proposed project. They are submitted for approval by the owner.

Secondary mortgage market. An unorganized market on which existing mortgages are bought and sold. It contrasts with the primary mortgage market, on which mortgages are originated.

Section. A drawing of an object or structure as it would appear if cut by an imaginary plane. Such a drawing is intended to show the internal arrangements and proportions of a structure.

Setback. The minimum distance allowed between a reference line (usually a property boundary) and a building's edge.

Shop drawings. Diagrams, illustrations, schedules, performance charts, and other data prepared by a manufacturer, supplier, or distributor to illustrate how specific materials or portions of work will be sized, fabricated, or installed.

Site analysis. The process of arriving at as complete a description as possible of the microclimate, surface, and subsurface features of a given property.

Site plan. A drawing prepared by the designer showing the property's boundaries and topographical features, which includes a proposed structure as it would be located on the property.

Skylight. An opening in a roof that is glazed with a transparent or translucent material. Functioning like a window, a skylight may be either operating or fixed. It is used to admit natural light to the space below and to provide ventilation if it is openable.

Soil boring. The process of securing soil samples for analysis. Penetration is generally to a depth several feet below the intended foundation depth of a proposed structure.

Soil test. An investigation of the properties of soil samples obtained by boring. Results of a test are usually accompanied by a written report including information concerning the type of soil, its depth, and bearing strength.

Solar heating and cooling. The development, design, construction, and operation of systems that use and/or store the radiant energy of sunlight to provide comfort control and heated water for household, industrial, or agricultural use.

Specifications (Specs). A part of the contract documents supplied by the designer. Specifications are written descriptions of a technical nature of the materials, equipment, construction systems, standards, and workmanship intended for a particular project. The list of specifications amplifies and explains the designer's plans and drawings.

Stock plans. House plans or designs, "in stock," intended to be used over and over. A potential owner can choose a stock plan and make minor alterations for taste or site, thereby saving some of the cost of custom design.

Subcontractor. A person or organization, such as a plumber or an electrician, who has a direct contract with the prime contractor to perform a portion of the work on a building project.

Survey. A description of the measure and marking of land, including maps and field notes that describe the property.

Sworn construction statement. A certified statement of the building contractor's estimation of the cost of construction, prepared before construction begins.

Thermal. Hot or warm.

Thermal break. An interruption in the heat flow along a highly conductive structural member. Such a break is provided by insulation placed at locations where a high-conductivity material such as concrete is in contact with both the inside and the outside of a structure. A typical location for a thermal break, for example, would be at the point where a concrete wall extends beyond an exposed wall.

Thermal storage. Retention of energy in the form of heat. Materials with capacity to retain or store heat are such "massive" substances as water, masonry, or rocks. Air has little mass and therefore little capacity for thermal storage.

Topography. The surface features of a place or region, including hills, valleys, streams, or lakes; or, an accurate description or drawing of places or their surface features.

Topping slab. A thin layer of concrete applied over a horizontal surface, such as a roof deck of precast concrete plant.

Treated wood. Wood that has been painted with, immersed in, or otherwise treated with a preservative. See also Pressure-treated wood.

Trombe wall. A passive solar heating system devised by Felix Trombe. A concrete wall with openings at the top and bottom is placed just inside south-facing glass. Air between the glass and the wall is heated by the sun, rising and entering the room behind through the Trombe wall's top opening. Cool air from the room flows to the space between the glass and wall through the bottom opening and is heated. The wall also stores heat and radiates it directly to the room behind.

Variance. A written authorization, from the responsible agency, permitting construction in a manner or place that is not otherwise allowed by code or other regulations.

Ventilation. The process of supplying or removing air, by natural or mechanical means, to or from any space.

Vent stack. A vertical pipe connected to the drainage system to allow ventilation and pressure equalization.

Vulcanized membranes. Waterproofing materials, including various natural and synthetic rubber compounds, that are formed into sheet membranes by vulcanization, a process that lends strength and resists cracking and deformation under stress. Examples are Butyl, EPDM, and neoprene.

Water table. The subsurface depth below which the ground is saturated.

Waterproof membrane. Thin, pliable, sheetlike materials for waterproofing. Examples of materials that come in membrane form are Butyl and neoprene. Asphalt alternated with felt or fabric reinforcing is an example of a built-up membrane comprised of several layers.

Waterproofing skin. Ranked in importance after good site planning and drainage, this is the third component in a good waterproofing system for an earth sheltered house. The skin may consist of several materials that work together to wrap the building in a moisture-proof shield.

Index